A2 Key for Schools Trainer

Six Practice Tests without answers

Second edition

Cambridge University Press
www.cambridge.org/elt
Cambridge Assessment English
www.cambridgeenglish.org

Information on this title: www.cambridge.org/9781108525817

© Cambridge University Press and UCLES 2019

This publication is in copyright. Subject to statutory exception and to the provisions of relevant collective licensing agreements, no reproduction of any part may take place without the written permission of Cambridge University Press.

First published 2018

20 19 18 17 16 15 14 13 12 11 10 9 8 7 6 5 4 3 2 1

Printed in Malaysia by Vivar Printing

A catalogue record for this publication is available from the British Library

ISBN 978-1-108-52581-7 Student's Book without answers with audio
ISBN 978-1-108-52580-0 Student's Book with answers with audio

The publishers have no responsibility for the persistence or accuracy of URLs for external or third-party internet websites referred to in this publication, and do not guarantee that any content on such websites is, or will remain, accurate or appropriate. Information regarding prices, travel timetables, and other factual information given in this work is correct at the time of first printing but the publishers do not guarantee the accuracy of such information thereafter.

It is normally necessary for written permission for copying to be obtained *in advance* from a publisher. The sample answer sheets at the back of this book are designed to be copied and distributed in class.

The normal requirements are waived here and it is not necessary to write to Cambridge University Press for permission for an individual teacher to make copies for use within his or her own classroom. Only those pages that carry the wording '© UCLES 2019 Photocopiable' may be copied.

Contents

Introduction			4

Training and Exam Practice

Test 1	Paper 1	Reading and Writing	10
	Paper 2	Listening	28
	Paper 3	Speaking	40
Test 2	Paper 1	Reading and Writing	44
	Paper 2	Listening	62
	Paper 3	Speaking	74

Practice Tests

Test 3	Paper 1	Reading and Writing	78
	Paper 2	Listening	88
	Paper 3	Speaking	154
Test 4	Paper 1	Reading and Writing	94
	Paper 2	Listening	104
	Paper 3	Speaking	154
Test 5	Paper 1	Reading and Writing	110
	Paper 2	Listening	120
	Paper 3	Speaking	155
Test 6	Paper 1	Reading and Writing	126
	Paper 2	Listening	136
	Paper 3	Speaking	155

Speaking frames Tests 1–6	142
Visual materials for Tests 3–6	154
Sample answer sheets	156
Acknowledgements	159

Introduction

If you are aged between 11 and 15 and want to take **A2 Key for Schools**, this book is for **YOU**!

This book is called '**Trainer**' because it is full of exercises to help you get better and better at doing each part of **A2 Key for Schools**.

So, complete all the exercises then do all the practice papers! If you train and work hard, you will soon be ready to take **A2 Key for Schools**!

First, do the exercises on each **Training** page.
Then do the task on the **Exam Practice** page and check your answers.

On Training pages, you will find:

 Cambridge Learner Corpus

This shows information about mistakes that some **A2 Key** candidates make. If you do these useful exercises, you will learn <u>not</u> to make these mistakes when you do **A2 Key for Schools**!

These are ideas to help you do well in the exam. For example: *Read the whole text. Try to understand what it says and why it was written.*

Remember

These are quick reminders about grammar points or vocabulary that you should learn. For example: *We use **is** with uncountable nouns, e.g. **air**, **money.***

On Exam Practice pages, you will find:

- an **A2 Key for Schools exam task** for you to try and complete
- further **tips** and **advice** to help you with different parts of the task

Tests 3, 4, 5 and 6

When you finish Tests 1 and 2, you will be ready to do complete **A2 Key for Schools practice tests**.

Tests 3, 4, 5 and 6 are just like real **A2 Key for Schools** Reading and Writing, Listening and Speaking papers. Doing these tests will help you even more to prepare for the exam.

Keep a record of your scores as you do the tests. You may find that your scores are good in some parts of the test, but you may need to practise other parts more. Make simple tables like this to help record your scores:

Paper 2 Listening

	Part 1	Part 2	Part 3	Part 4	Part 5
Test 3					
Test 4					
Test 5					
Test 6					

Other features of the *A2 Key for Schools Trainer*

- **Visual material**
  In the Speaking test, the examiner will give you some written information. The visual material on pages 154-155 will help you practise and become familiar with the type of information you will be given and help you increase your confidence.

- **Sample answer sheets**
  Look at these to see what the *A2 Key for Schools* answer sheets in the test look like and learn how to complete them. Ask your teacher to photocopy them so that you can use them when you do practice tests.

- **Downloadable audio online**
  Listen to these to practise the Listening paper. You will also need to listen to these to complete some of the Speaking Training exercises and to hear a demonstration of each part of the Speaking paper.

The structure of the *A2 Key for Schools* exam

The *A2 Key for Schools* exam has three papers:

Reading and Writing: 1 hour
You will need to able to read and understand simple information that you might see on signs or read in brochures, newspaper or magazine articles. You will also have to choose words to fill gaps in a text and complete a text with your own words. You will have to write a short note or email that is a minimum of 25 words and a short story or description about three sequenced pictures of 35 words or more.

Listening: 30 minutes
You will need to be able to listen to and understand people who are talking together or people who are giving information about something. You will have to choose or write answers to questions which are about what these people say. Don't worry! The people talk very clearly and they don't talk fast!

Speaking: 8–10 minutes (13–15 minutes for three candidates)
You will need to be able to listen and understand what the examiner is saying. You will have to answer some simple questions about yourself. You will also be given some pictures to look at. You will talk about the pictures with another candidate and the examiner. You will then answer some more questions about the topic. You usually take the Speaking test with just one other candidate, but sometimes candidates take the Speaking test in groups of three.

Frequently asked questions

Is my English good enough for A2 Key for Schools?

The level of the tests is Council of Europe Level A2. At A2 level, *Key* students can:
- understand simple instructions and questions
- write, talk or ask about simple information, opinions or ideas
- complete forms
- write short, simple letters, messages or emails about personal information.

For more information on 'Can Do' statements go to:
https://www.cambridgeenglish.org/exams-and-tests/cefr

Note that some candidates might be better than others (at speaking or writing, for example), but still get the same final **A2 Key for Schools** grade. The A2 'Can Do' statements therefore help teachers to understand what **A2 Key** candidates should generally be able to do at this level.

What percentage grade do I need to get to pass A2 Key for Schools?

The percentage of marks that candidates need to get for each grade may change from test to test. This is because tests cannot always be exactly the same. Some might be a little more difficult than others. However, the ranges of percentages for each grade of **A2 Key for Schools** are:
- Pass with Merit 85%, i.e. 85 out of 100 marks
- Pass 70% — 84%
- Narrow Fail 65% — 69%
- Fail 64% and below.

This information is included on your Statement of Results.

> What marks do I need to pass each paper, and to pass the exam?

Candidates do not have to get a certain mark to pass each section of the test. The final mark for **A2 Key for Schools** is the total number of marks from all three papers: Reading and Writing, Listening and Speaking. There are an equal number of possible marks for Reading and Writing, Listening and Speaking at **A2 Key for Schools**.

> Is A2 Key for Schools suitable for candidates of any age?

A2 Key for Schools is more suitable for students who are at school and aged from 11 to 15. To make sure that the material is not too difficult or too easy for this age group, all the parts of the Reading and Writing and Listening papers are pre-tested. This means that different groups of students try each part of the tests first. The parts will then only be used in real exams if the results of the tests show they are suitable for candidates who want to take **A2 Key for Schools**.

> Can I use pens and pencils?

In **A2 Key** and **A2 Key for Schools**, candidates must use **pencil** in all papers.

What happens if I don't have enough time to finish writing?

You can only be given marks for what you write on your answer sheets, so if you cannot complete this, you will lose marks. Watch the clock, plan your time carefully and do not waste time by writing answers on other pieces of paper first. If you want to change an answer, just rub it out, write your correct answer then quickly move to the next question.

If I write in capital letters, will this affect my score?

No. You do not lose marks for writing in capital letters in **A2 Key for Schools**. Whether you choose to use capital letters or not, you should always make sure that your handwriting is clear and easy to read. Remember that the examiners can't mark a piece of writing that they can't read!

Training Test 1 — Reading and Writing Part 1

In this part, you:
- **read** six notices, emails or messages
- **answer** a multiple-choice question about each text

VOCABULARY: FOCUS ON MEANING

1 Look at the pairs of words and phrases. Write *S* for those with similar meanings and *D* for those with different meanings.

   Example: entrance / door ..S..
   1 on foot / walk ....
   2 picnic / fast food ....
   3 on time / late ....
   4 pupils / students ....
   5 instead / as well ....
   6 by car / drive ....
   7 lend / borrow ....
   8 forest / wood ....

TIP Part 1 uses different ways to say the same thing. A word or phrase in the notice, email or message might have the same meaning as a different word or phrase in the question.

2 Now complete the sentences with some of the words from Exercise 1.

   Example: We got lost in the ....forest..... There are so many trees!
   1 Summer .... 3 p.m. in Arnos Park. Bring your own food!
   2 Hi Jack, I can't come on Monday. Can we meet on Tuesday ....?
   3 Bus leaves at 8 a.m. Please be ....
   4 Students who .... to school must change their shoes.
   5 Pupils who need to .... a hockey stick should come to the gym at 1:15.

3 Who CANNOT do each activity? Use two words from the box for each notice.

| children | teenagers | adults |

Example: This film is for adults only. ......*children*...... and ......*teenagers*......

1 Play area for under 8s only. .... and ....
2 Art competition for 13–19 year-olds. .... and ....
3 Holidays for 20–35 year-olds. .... and ....
4 Kids' bike race. No-one over 12 please! .... and ....

TIP Words about age, like *adult*, *child* and *teenager*, are often tested in Part 1.

GRAMMAR: MODAL VERBS

4 Read the notices. Complete the sentences with words from the box.

| ~~can't~~ | can | must | need | should | will |

TIP Questions about notices often use words such as *can*, *will*, *must*, *might* and *should*. Make sure you know what they mean.

Example: No credit cards under £5.

You ......*can't*...... use a credit card if you spend less than £5.

Free entry for under 8s.

1 Younger children don't .... to pay.

No talking in the library!

2 You .... be quiet in the library.

German spoken here.

3 Staff .... speak German.

Please give your seat to those who need it.

4 You .... offer your seat to others.

Discounts for members.

5 Members .... pay less.

Reading and Writing Part 1

Exam Practice Test 1 — Reading and Writing Part 1

Questions 1–6

For each question, choose the correct answer.

1

> Please note:
> this afternoon's football class
> will be tomorrow instead,
> as Mr Hall is away today.

A There is no football class today.

B Mr Hall can't come to the football class tomorrow.

C You can choose to go to the football class today or tomorrow.

2

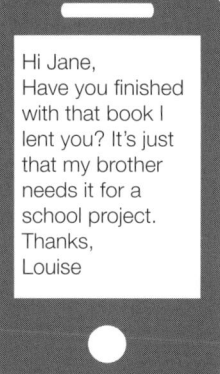

Hi Jane,
Have you finished with that book I lent you? It's just that my brother needs it for a school project.
Thanks,
Louise

A Louise is offering to lend Jane a book.

B Louise wants her book back from Jane.

C Louise's brother has borrowed a book from Jane.

3

Picnic area
No ball games here – please use the other side of the park.

A You can buy food somewhere else in the park.

B Please don't eat while you are playing sport here.

C This is a place for eating and you can't play football here.

Advice

1 If something is happening **this afternoon**, is it happening today or tomorrow?

2 Why do you think Jane says **Have you finished with that book?**

3 What can't you do here?

5 If you **come on foot**, how do you travel?

4

A Adults can take children to the museum in the morning.

B Adults with children over 12 will enjoy the museum.

C Children can visit the museum if they are with an adult.

5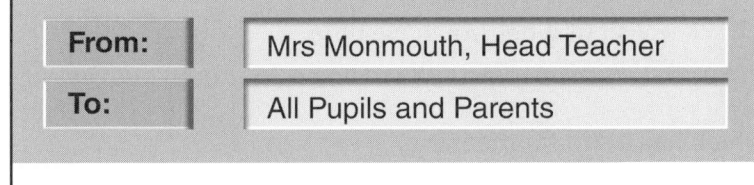

Hello,

This week, please don't use the car to get to school. Coming on foot is healthy and doesn't take much time.

Thanks,
Mrs Monmouth

Why has Mrs Monmouth written this message?

A to ask pupils to walk to school

B to tell pupils to get to school on time

C to explain about a health problem at school

6

A Pedro's Pizza Bar isn't open at weekends.

B The third time you visit, you get a free pizza.

C Three pizzas cost the same as two.

Training Test 1 — Reading and Writing Part 2

In this part, you:
- **read**   three texts on a similar topic
- **match**   sentences to the texts

TIP The text and question about it will give the same idea in different words. Read the whole sentence and text carefully to see if the meaning is the same or different.

VOCABULARY: FOCUS ON MEANING

1   Match each sentence 1–5 with another way of saying the same thing.

Example: Town is always busy at the weekend.   The things we have here are always changing.
1. Learn about the world.   Someone will have to show you around.
2. You can come as often as you want.   You will be able to look at the clothes worn by the workers.
3. You can see something different every time.   Find out about different places.
4. You can see what the staff had to wear.   Visit us when you have time.
5. You will need to have a guide.   *Lots of people go shopping on Saturdays and Sundays.*

2   Read the sentence and tick (✓) the sentence which has a similar meaning.

Example: The museum is open every day except Sunday.
- **A** The museum is closed on Sundays.   ✓
- **B** The museum will open on Sunday.   ☐

1. A family ticket is for two adults and up to three children.
   - **A** Adults and children have to buy a ticket. ☐
   - **B** Five people can go in on the same ticket. ☐
2. The café serves teas, coffees, cakes and biscuits.
   - **A** You can have a drink and snack at the café. ☐
   - **B** You can have a meal at the café. ☐
3. The best time to visit is the summer.
   - **A** You should come when it's warmer. ☐
   - **B** It's really nice in the winter months. ☐

 A2 Key candidates often make mistakes with modals such as *can*, *should* and *have to*.

GRAMMAR: *THERE IS* AND *THERE ARE*

3 Cross out the wrong word in each sentence.

> **Remember**
> We use *is* with uncountable nouns, e.g. *air*, *money*.

Example: There **is** / ~~are~~ *a sofa in the living room.*
1 There *is* / *are* too many people in our city.
2 There *is* / *are* a lot of advice on the website.
3 There *is* / *are* some letters for you.
4 There *is* / *are* no water in the swimming pool.
5 There *is* / *are* snakes in the grass.

Exam Practice Test 1 — Reading and Writing Part 2

Questions 7–13

For each question, choose the correct answer.

		Eureka!	Museum of Museums	Cinema Museum
7	Which museum has an exhibition of clothes?	A	B	C
8	Which museum is full of things which visitors can touch?	A	B	C
9	Which museum is a good place to learn about how people travelled in the past?	A	B	C
10	Which museum can you visit again for free after you pay once?	A	B	C
11	Which museum do you need to contact before you visit?	A	B	C
12	Which museum shows things that were borrowed from other places?	A	B	C
13	Which museum has some furniture which wasn't needed any more?	A	B	C

Advice

8 How else can you say **touch**?

9 Think of some things that people can travel in.

10 Can you think of other ways to say **for free**?

12 Which other word has a similar meaning to **borrow**?

Three museums

Eureka!

Eureka! is a complete hands-on experience, which means that visitors can actually pick up any object in the museum. It's a great way for young visitors to learn about the world, the body, how things work and move. And when you buy an entry ticket, it allows you to come back as many times as you want for a whole year for no extra cost. As Eureka! is right next to Halifax train station, it's very easy to get to from all over the country.

Museum of Museums

Every time you visit the Museum of Museums, you'll be able to see something different. And that's because the things you see there are actually lent by other museums around the country. The museum always has lots of different vehicles, from ice-cream vans and old motorbikes to the different kinds of public transport people used to get to work many years ago. You can find out about all this and lots more.

Cinema Museum

Ronald Grant, who opened the Cinema Museum in the 1960s, travelled round the country and bought things from cinemas which were closing down. This included old film posters and wooden cinema seating. At the museum, you can now see these and much more, including the uniforms that cinema staff once had to wear.

Please let us know by phone or email if you'd like to come. We'll be happy to see you, but we need to arrange a guide, as it's only possible to visit the museum on an organised tour.

Training Test 1 — Reading and Writing Part 3

In this part, you:
- **read** a text
- **answer** five multiple-choice questions

VOCABULARY: FOCUS ON MEANING

1 Read the text and choose the best title.

 TIP For some questions you need to understand the main, or most important, idea. Read the text from start to finish. Think about what information is very important and which is less important.

We are looking for students to join the school band. You don't need to know how to play an instrument yet. We will teach you! Choose from the guitar, drums or keyboard. You don't need to buy your own instrument, as the school will lend you one. You can even take it home to practise. All we need is your time – one hour a week for a music lesson on Monday or Tuesday, and two hours on Thursday evening for band practice. So, come along and have some fun!

A Types of music B Free music lessons C Join the band!

2 Now choose the correct answer about the text in Exercise 1.

1 The school band is looking for
  A students who can play an instrument.
  B students who want to join the band.
  C students who have their own instrument.

2 Band practice
  A is on Thursday.
  B is on Monday or Tuesday.
  C lasts one hour.

 TIP In the exam underline the words to help you choose the correct answer.

Which words helped you to choose your answers? Underline them.

GRAMMAR: *IN*, *SINCE*, *FOR* AND *AGO*

3 Complete the sentences with *in*, *since*, *for* or *ago*.

   Example: I've known Marcus ......*for*...... a long time.

   1 We first met .... 2010.
   2 I visited Australia five years ....
   3 My parents have lived here .... the early 2000s.
   4 I spoke to my teacher a few minutes ....
   5 I love going to the beach .... the summer.
   6 We study English .... an hour each day.
   7 It's a few years .... I last saw him.

Exam Practice Test 1 — Reading and Writing Part 3

Questions 14–18

For each question, choose the correct answer.

Will's blog

One day my dad said, 'Why don't we have a street party?' This means that the street is closed so cars can't use it, and people put tables and chairs out in the street, then have a party! Dad said there was one in 1977 and he still remembers it well. Everyone loved it! I couldn't believe that since 1977 they never had another one. If it was so good, why not do it again?

We started to organise it, together with some other people. I helped to make the web page, so everyone on the street knew about the party and could post their old photos from the party in 1977. There were some pictures of my dad when he was a kid, together with his friends, who have moved away from the street now. It was interesting to see that the buildings on the street haven't changed at all!

My mum was a bit worried about the party. 'But a lot of people on the street don't really know each other', she said. 'What if they don't have anything to talk about?' I just said, 'Relax, Mum. It'll be great.'

So, what was the party like? It was fantastic! My friends and I really liked speaking to an old lady called Louisa. She's 89 and was telling us about when she and her friends were our age. So now I always chat to her when I see her on the street. I didn't know who she was before, so I'm glad we had the party.

---

14 Why was Will surprised?
   A   His father wanted to have a street party.
   B   There hasn't been a street party for a long time.
   C   Many people remembered the last street party.

15 What did the photos from 1977 show?
   A   The street still looks the same now.
   B   There are more children living in the street now.
   C   The same people still live on the street now.

16 Why was Will's mother worried?
   A   She thought that the party was too expensive.
   B   She thought that people might not come to the party.
   C   She thought that the guests might not talk to each other.

17 Will and his friends enjoyed
   A   hearing Louisa's stories.
   B   meeting Louisa's friends.
   C   telling Louisa about their lives.

18 What is the best title for the article?
   A   Why I love street parties
   B   The street party we had
   C   How to have a street party

Advice

14 *What does Will say he **couldn't believe**?*

16 *What did Will's mother actually say?*

18 *Which information (A, B or C) is in every paragraph?*

Training Test 1 — Reading and Writing Part 4

In this part, you:
- **read**   a text with six gaps
- **choose**   answers from A, B or C for each gap

GRAMMAR: PRESENT SIMPLE

1 **Cross out the wrong word in each sentence.**

   Example: Camels **live** / ~~**lives**~~ *in the desert.*

  1 Sea water *is* / *are* full of salt.
  2 Elephants *don't* / *doesn't* eat meat.
  3 That man *come* / *comes* from London.
  4 It *isn't* / *aren't* very far to my school.
  5 Cities *has* / *have* better transport than villages.
  6 Grass *grow* / *grows* faster in summer.
  7 My country *don't* / *doesn't* have many lakes.

VOCABULARY: FOCUS ON MEANING

2 **Choose the best word for each space.**

   Example: I haven't been to the new …A… centre.

    A shopping   **B** shop   **C** buying

  1 Lily has her ………… bicycle.
    A even   **B** one   **C** own

  2 The park is ………… for the winter.
    A closed   **B** finished   **C** ended

  3 Dinosaurs ………… all over the world.
    A spent   **B** lived   **C** took

  4 The driver told everyone to get ………… the bus when we arrived.
    A off   **B** up   **C** down

  5 The ………… was quite difficult.
    A instructions   **B** mark   **C** test

> **TIP**   The words you have to choose from will be quite similar, e.g. size, area or space. They will also all be nouns, adverbs, prepositions, verbs, etc. Read the sentence carefully with each word in the gap before you choose one.

3 **Read the text. Cross out the wrong words in each sentence.**
  1 The text is *fact* / *a story*.
  2 It comes from *an advertisement* / *a book*.
  3 It is in the *present simple* / *past simple* tense.

> **TIP**   Read the whole text. Try to understand what it says and why it was written.

Bees are flying insects. There are around 20,000 different types of bees in the world. Most bees live in large groups, but some live alone. They use flowers to make honey, which is also their food. There are many worker bees, but only one queen bee in every large group. All the other bees have to look after her. Most bees live between 40 days and 5 months, but queen bees live for about 3 years.

4 Now find words with these meanings in the text in Exercise 3.

Example: kinds ......types......

1 big ....
2 without other (bees) ....
3 a lot of ....
4 care for ....

Exam Practice Test 1 — Reading and Writing Part 4

Questions 19–24

For each question, choose the correct answer.

Red pandas

Red pandas live in Nepal, Northern Myanmar, India and Bhutan, as **(19)** .... as in China. They **(20)** .... a lot of their time in trees and are very **(21)** .... at climbing. They are more active during the night than the day, and they usually **(22)** .... for food in the evening and early in the morning. Their favourite food is bamboo. In fact, a female red panda can eat 20,000 bamboo leaves in a day! But they also eat fruit, grass, eggs, insects and **(23)** .... small birds and animals. Scientists believe that the number of red pandas in the world is **(24)** .... because the forests where they live are getting smaller. But much is being done in countries around the world to help this amazing animal.

19 A soon   B much   C well
20 A spend   B live   C take
21 A nice   B great   C good
22 A look   B see   C find
23 A even   B quite   C still
24 A little   B low   C short

Advice

20 What verb can you use with **time**: to .... time?
21 If you can do something well (e.g. cooking), you can say that you are .... **at cooking**.
22 Which verb goes before **for**: **look**, **see** or **find**?

Training Test 1 — Reading and Writing Part 5

In this part, you:
- **read** one or two emails
- **write** six missing words

VOCABULARY: FOCUS ON MEANING

1 Match the parts of the phrases.

Example: Thank you for — your help.
1. That was very — kind of you.
2. I'm sorry — to see you.
3. What's — the weather like?
4. I can't wait — to see you.
5. Can I — help you?
6. I'm very — pleased for you.
7. See you — soon.

> **TIP** In Part 5, the missing word is sometimes part of a phrase, such as *What's the weather like?*, so try and learn fixed phrases.

👁 *A2 Key* candidates often make mistakes with words like **on**, **at** and **in** when they are writing about times, days and dates.

GRAMMAR: PREPOSITIONS

2 Correct the mistakes. Write the correct preposition.

Example: Jeff Kinney was born **in** 19th February 1971. ......on......
1. Kinney is <u>of</u> Maryland, USA. ....
2. His book *Diary of a Wimpy Kid* is read <u>for</u> 70,000 children every day. ....
3. In college, he wrote <u>about</u> the school newspaper. ....
4. Kinney moved <u>at</u> Massachusetts in 1997. ....
5. He enjoys spending time <u>among</u> his two children. ....

> **TIP** Prepositions are often tested in Part 5. Learn which words they go with.

GRAMMAR: ADVERBS

3 Complete the sentences with words from the box.

| yet | even | before | soon | quite | ~~well~~ | just |

Example: Sandesh can play the guitar as ......well...... as the piano.
1. Haven't you done your homework ....? It's for tomorrow!
2. I've never eaten Mexican food .... It's really nice.
3. I've .... spoken to the teacher. She says we can have more time.
4. The film was .... funny, wasn't it?
5. I ate everything – .... the vegetables!
6. We need to leave .... or we will be late.

> **TIP** Adverbs are also often tested in Part 5. Make sure you know what each one means and how it is used.

Exam Practice Test 1 — Reading and Writing Part 5

Questions 25–30

For each question, write the correct answer.
Write **ONE** word for each gap.

Example: **0** MUCH

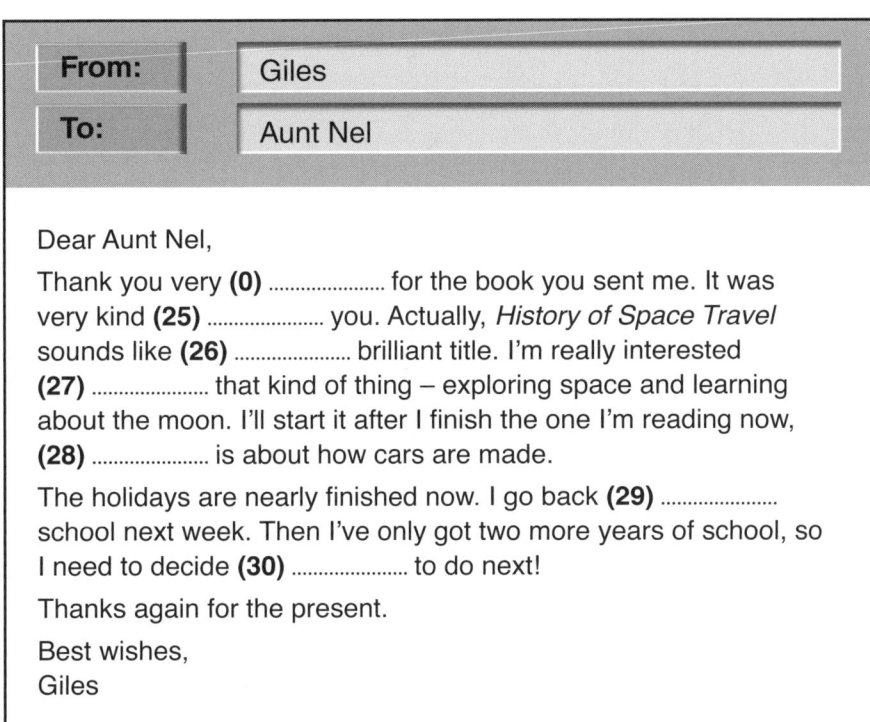

Dear Aunt Nel,

Thank you very **(0)** .... for the book you sent me. It was very kind **(25)** .... you. Actually, *History of Space Travel* sounds like **(26)** .... brilliant title. I'm really interested **(27)** .... that kind of thing – exploring space and learning about the moon. I'll start it after I finish the one I'm reading now, **(28)** .... is about how cars are made.

The holidays are nearly finished now. I go back **(29)** .... school next week. Then I've only got two more years of school, so I need to decide **(30)** .... to do next!

Thanks again for the present.

Best wishes,
Giles

Advice

27 *What word is often used after interested?*

29 *Where will Giles go next week?*

Training Test 1 — Reading and Writing Part 6

In this part, you:
- **read** — an email or some bullet points
- **write** — an email

VOCABULARY: FOCUS ON MEANING

1   Read the questions and answers. Decide if each answer is correct for that question. If the answer is right, put a tick (✓). If it is wrong, put a cross (✗).

	Example: Which film would you like to see?	I went to see 'Silver Moon'.	✗
1	Which day are we going to play tennis?	We're playing tennis on Thursday.	
2	Where did you go on holiday?	We're flying to Paris.	
3	Who do you think will be there?	Most of our class are going.	
4	Why did you like the film?	It was very exciting.	
5	What time does the class start?	It began at 10 o'clock.	
6	What do you usually do at the weekend?	I went shopping.	
7	When do you want me to meet you?	I think I'll be finished by 4 o'clock.	
8	How are we going to get there?	We'll go by bus.	

2   Look at this example of a Part 6 task. Underline the three pieces of information that you will need to write in the answer.

From: Jake
To: Mattie

Hi Mattie,

A new swimming pool has opened five minutes' walk from the school. Let's go sometime next week. Which day is best for you? The pool is open from 10 a.m. to 10 p.m. What time of day shall we go? Do you want to ask any of the other students to come with us?

Bye,
Jake

3   Read the three short messages. Match each message with one of Jake's questions from Exercise 2.

1. Hi Mattie,
I think Claudia and Petra would like to go swimming with us.

2. Hi!
We could go after the class, so we have more time.

3. Dear Mattie,
I'm not doing anything on Wednesday next week.

1 ....
2 ....
3 ....

24   Training Test 1   Reading and Writing Part 6

GRAMMAR: -ING FORMS

4 Write the -ing form of the verb in brackets. Use *Remember* to help you.

Example: My sister loves (shop) for new clothes. ......shopping......

1. Are you (go) to the beach at the weekend? ....
2. That man is (run) for the bus! ....
3. My brothers are (study) at university. ....
4. My uncle is (drive) me to the airport. ....
5. My mum is (buy) some bread. ....
6. I'm (get) up early tomorrow. ....
7. Sami often goes (ice-skate) in winter. ....

Remember

Verbs ending in a vowel or -y don't change, e.g. *play* → *playing*, *try* → *trying*. You simply add -ing.

For verbs that end in -e, take off the -e before -ing, e.g. *dance* → *dancing*, *write* → *writing*.

Double the final consonant when a one-syllable verb ends in consonant + vowel + consonant, e.g. *stop* → *stopping*, *swim* → *swimming*.

Exam Practice Test 1 — Reading and Writing Part 6

Question 31

Read this email from your English friend, Francis.

From:	Francis
To:	
Subject:	This weekend

Hi,

It's great that you're free to meet me this weekend. I have a few questions. Where is the best place in your town to meet? What would you like to do? And shall I bring anything?

Write soon!
Francis

Write an email to Francis and answer his questions.
Write **25 words** or more.
Write the email on your answer sheet.

Advice

How many questions does Francis ask?

Make sure you answer them all!

Remember to say something friendly to Francis at the start or the end of your email.

Training Test 1 — Reading and Writing Part 7

In this part, you:
- **look** at three pictures
- **write** a short story

VOCABULARY: FOCUS ON MEANING

1 Write the words in the correct column.

boat	by sea	car park	flight	garage	landing	motorway	pilot	platform
railway	roundabout	sail	ship	station	take off	train	tram	

Rail	Water	Car	Air
	boat		

GRAMMAR: PAST TENSES

2 Find nine other past tense verbs in the wordsearch. Then write the present tense form of the words.

C	W	F	A	T	T	O	O	K	B	I	U	A
A	T	E	M	O	C	M	L	O	R	E	T	A
U	N	L	E	J	A	P	O	D	I	D	Y	L
G	K	P	W	P	M	A	R	H	G	F	W	E
H	B	R	O	K	E	B	E	L	O	L	P	F
T	E	R	N	I	O	G	S	E	T	P	U	T

Example: broke – break

3 Now complete the sentences with some of the words from Exercise 2.

Example: Betty ..broke.. the window.

1 The children .... sandwiches and apples.
2 The boy .... the race.
3 Terrie .... a photograph of his brother.
4 The younger boy .... the ball.
5 The girl .... her bag on the chair.
6 Kim .... really well in his exam.
7 Susan .... a new dress yesterday.

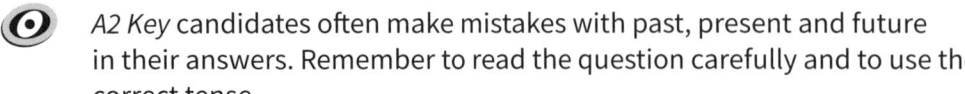 *A2 Key* candidates often make mistakes with past, present and future in their answers. Remember to read the question carefully and to use the correct tense.

FUNCTIONAL LANGUAGE: DESCRIPTION

4 Look at the pictures. Think of your own answers to the questions.

TIP Look at the pictures and think of the words you will need. Think of the past tense forms of the verbs.

Where were the people?
What was the boy's name?
Who were the man and woman?

What were they doing?
What did the boy do on the train?
How did the boy feel?

5 Read what Elena and Carlos wrote about the pictures in Exercise 4. Which answer is better? Why?

> Elena
>
> Thursday afternoon Pablo went by train. Pablo was very happy. His parents came to station say goodbye to Pablo. He ate sandwich and apple. He drank water. He read a book about dinosaurs.

> Carlos
>
> A boy went on a train. He went to some place. A man and woman say goodbye to boy. Boy ate food. He drank something.

Exam Practice Test 1 — Reading and Writing Part 7

Question 32

Look at the three pictures.
Write the story shown in the pictures.
Write **35 words** or more.

Advice
You should use past tenses to tell your story.

Write the story on your answer sheet.

Training Test 1 — Listening Part 1

In this part, you:
- **read** five questions and **look at** three possible picture answers
- **listen** to five short conversations and **choose** the right answer (A, B or C) for each

VOCABULARY: DESCRIBING PEOPLE

1 Who do these words describe? Write *T* (Tom), *A* (Axel) or *N* (Niko).

Example: tall ....T....

1	blonde	....	8 coat	....
2	short	....	9 dark hair	....
3	beard	....	10 long hair	....
4	T-shirt	....	11 shorts	....
5	fat	....	12 trousers	....
6	short hair	....	13 jeans	....
7	slim	....	14 shirt	....

Tom

Axel

Niko

 2 Who is the woman describing? Listen and choose the correct answer in Exercise 1.

VOCABULARY: PARTS OF THE HOME

3 Label the pictures with words from the box.

| armchair | cooker | television | sink | sofa | bookcase |
| ~~lamp~~ | pillow | bed | fridge | cupboard | desk |

A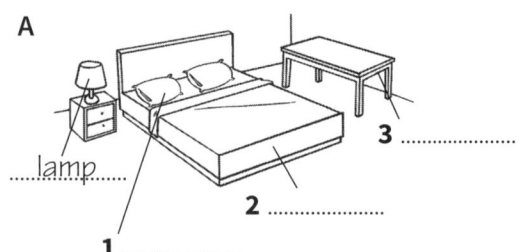
lamp, 1 ...., 2 ...., 3 ....

B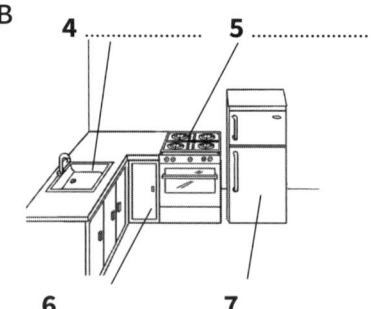
4 ...., 5 ...., 6 ...., 7 ....

C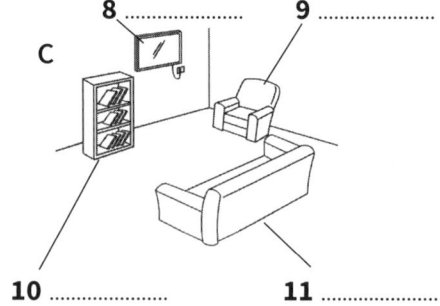
8 ...., 9 ...., 10 ...., 11 ....

4 Look at the pictures in Exercise 3. If the sentence is right, put a tick (✓). If it is wrong, put a cross (✗).

Example: The lamp is on the table next to the bed. ✓
1 The pillow is under the bed. ☐
2 The bookcase is between the armchair and the sofa. ☐
3 The desk is against the wall. ☐
4 The fridge is next to the cooker. ☐
5 The lamp is in the living room. ☐
6 There is a cupboard under the sink. ☐

GRAMMAR: FUTURE FORMS

5 Listen to the sentences and decide if they are about the present or the future. Write *P* (present) or *F* (future).

Example: ....P....

1 ....   3 ....   5 ....   7 ....
2 ....   4 ....   6 ....   8 ....

6 When are they going to play tennis? Listen and choose the correct answer.

A Saturday   B Sunday   C Thursday

VOCABULARY: SUGGESTIONS

TIP When you hear a speaker making a suggestion, listen carefully to how the other speaker replies. Do they agree or not?

7 Match each suggestion with two possible replies.

Example: Let's go to the park.
1 What about having a chocolate cake?
2 Shall we go by train?
3 We could ask Paula to help.

No, let's drive. ....
I would prefer coffee. ....
Yes, that sounds delicious. ....
Good idea. She's really clever. ....
Yes, and let's take a ball. ....
She's very busy at the moment. ....
It's just started to rain. ....D....
Fine. It's only a 5-minute walk to the station. ....A....

8 Is each reply in Exercise 7 used to agree or disagree with the suggestion? Write *A* (agree) or *D* (disagree) next to each reply.

9 Where do they agree to have coffee? Listen and choose the correct answer.

A   B   C

Exam Practice Test 1 — Listening Part 1

Questions 1–5
05 For each question, choose the correct answer.

1 Where's the girl going this afternoon?

A

B

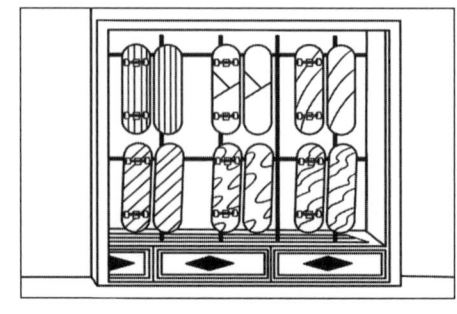
C

2 Which is the boy's new desk?

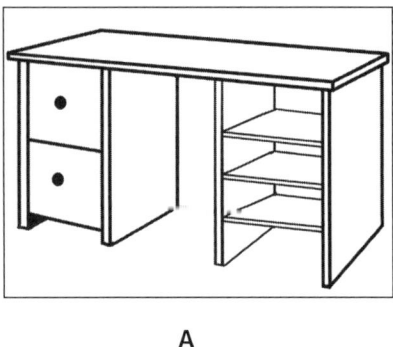
A

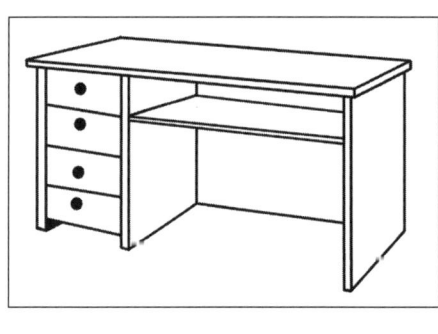
B

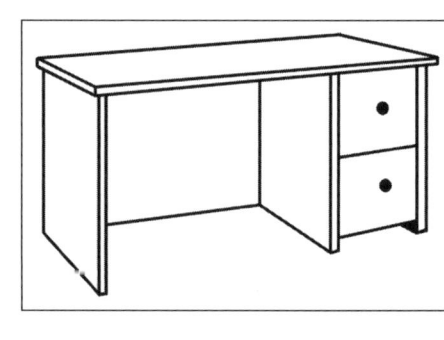
C

3 How will they get to their tennis class?

A

B

C

4 Which woman is Laura's new English teacher?

A

B

C

5 What might Harry do if it rains on Saturday?

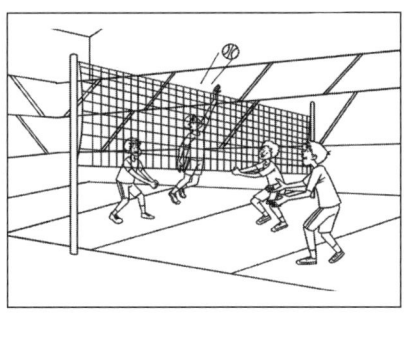
A

B

C

Advice

1 *Read the question carefully! It's asking about the girl (not the boy or his mum).*

3 *Listen until the end of the conversation before you choose the answer. Here the answer comes when you hear* Good idea.

Training Test 1 — Listening Part 2

In this part, you:
- **listen** to one speaker giving information
- **write** words in five gaps in some notes

VOCABULARY: TIME

1 Match the clocks with two times from the box.

one forty-five	~~midday~~	twenty past three
~~twelve noon~~	half six	quarter to two	five thirty
half past five	six thirty	three twenty

Remember
There are different ways of saying times. Make sure you know what they are.

Example: 1   2   3   4

..... midday .....
..... twelve noon .....

2 When do the friends agree to meet? Listen and choose the correct answer.

06

A    B    C

3 Look at the notes in Exercise 4 and answer the questions.
1 What will the recording be about? ....
2 You need to write two different times. What are they? ....
3 Can you think of other words for *start* and *finish*? ....
4 Which answer do you think will give the spelling? ....
5 What are two words that might go in gap 4? ....

TIP Read the notes carefully before you listen. Look at the words before and after the gaps. What kind of information will you write in each one?

4 Listen and complete the notes.

07

End-of-term dinner

Date:	28th March
Start time:	(1) ....
Finish time:	(2) ....
Place:	(3) .... restaurant
Menu:	Fish, chicken or vegetable (4) ....
Phone number:	(5) ....

Exam Practice Test 1 — Listening Part 2

Questions 6–10

For each question, write the correct answer in the gap. Write **one word** or **a number** or **a date** or **a time**.

You will hear a teacher talking to a class about a new music club.

New music club

Start date:	15th September
Day club will meet:	(6) ....
Time:	(7) from .... to 5 p.m.
Teacher's name:	(8) Mr ....
Teacher's phone number:	(9) ....
Place:	(10) ....

Advice

6 You hear **Wednesdays** and **Thursdays**, but which day is the Music Club?

7 What are other ways you can say **the club is from ... to 5 p.m.**?

8 When you see **name**, you should listen carefully, as this often means you have to spell the word.

9 In phone numbers, **double** means you have to write the number twice.

Training Test 1 — Listening Part 3

In this part, you:
- **read** five questions
- **listen** to a conversation and **choose** the correct answer (A, B or C)

VOCABULARY: FAMILY MEMBERS

1 Complete the sentences with the correct family member.

Example: My mother's brother is my ......uncle...... .

1 My aunt's children are my ....
2 I'm a girl. I'm my parents' ....
3 My father's mother is my ....
4 My parents' son is my ....
5 The man my sister is married to is her ....

2 Who is the girl talking about? Listen and choose the correct answer.

A Her father   B Her grandfather   C Her uncle

VOCABULARY: OPPOSITES

3 Complete the sentences with words from the box.

| sick | good | ~~hard~~ | slow | soft | old |

Example: A: The test wasn't very easy, was it?
B: No, it was quite ......hard...... .

1 A: How is Martina? Is she well?
   B: No, she's been .... for a few days.
2 A: Is that a new bicycle?
   B: Yes, I gave my .... one to my brother.
3 The internet is really fast here. It's so .... at my house.
4 A: The weather is so bad today.
   B: Yes, it's not very ...., is it?
5 This pillow is very hard. I like .... pillows.

TIP It is useful to know opposite words as the words you hear may be different from the words in the question.

GRAMMAR: GIVING PREFERENCES

4 Complete the conversation with words from the box. Then listen and check your answers.

| best | most | prefer | ~~favourite~~ | least |

Lucia: What's your (0) ......favourite...... food?
Marc: Umm, well, I love spicy food the (1) .... What about you?
Lucia: I (2) .... sweet food, like cakes and biscuits.
Marc: But you can't eat that for dinner!
Lucia: Well, fish is my (3) .... favourite meal. Apart from that, I'll eat anything.
Marc: Really? Fish is one of the things I like (4) ....

Exam Practice Test 1 — Listening Part 3

 Questions 11–15

For each question, choose the correct answer.

You will hear Luis talking to his friend Charlotte about a computer game.

11 Where did Luis first find out about the game?
   A from a game website
   B from a school friend
   C from a magazine advertisement

12 Charlotte likes the game because
   A it's funny.
   B it's hard.
   C it's new.

13 Who does Luis want to play the game with?
   A his brother
   B his granddad
   C his cousin

14 How long did Charlotte play the game for last Saturday?
   A forty-five minutes
   B one hour
   C one hour and thirty minutes

15 Which part of the game does Luis like best?
   A finding food
   B building a hut
   C crossing the river

Advice

11 Read the question carefully. The word **first** is very important.

12 Sometimes the question and the recording use words that are opposites. What are the opposites of **funny**, **hard** and **new**?

14 There are other ways to say these times, e.g. **one hour** is the same as saying **sixty minutes**.

15 Listen for words on the recording that mean the same as important words in the question, e.g. **like best**.

Training Test 1 Listening Part 4

In this part, you:
- **read** five questions
- **listen** to one person talking or a conversation and **choose** the correct answer

VOCABULARY: THINGS YOU DO

1 Write the words in the correct column.

bracelet   sausages   cricket   newspapers   the drums   mushrooms   video games
magazines   sports kit   perfume   fish   web page   tights   hockey   biscuit   comic

Things you eat	Things you wear	Things you play	Things you read
	bracelet		

2 Now complete the sentences with some of the words from Exercise 1.

Example: When it's cold, girls often wear ......tights.......

1 I like to have a .... with my cup of tea.
2 My parents gave me a gold .... for my birthday.
3 Now most people go online to read the news. Not many people buy ....
4 You can play .... on grass or on ice.
5 We change into our .... before we play football.

👁 *A2 Key* candidates often make mistakes when they write vowels (*a, e, i, o, u*) that they hear. Make sure you know how these are said in English.

VOCABULARY: SPELLING

3 Listen. Are these words and phrases spelt correctly? If the spelling is right, put a tick (✓). If it is wrong, put a cross (✗).

Example: Mrs Payne ✓   3 Montclaire ☐
1 Brookdale Street ☐   4 Simone Jordan ☐
2 The Penridge Room ☐   5 www.tourseylon.com ☐

Remember
When someone says *double* before a letter, you write the letter twice.

VOCABULARY: DATES

4 Listen and write the date you hear.

Example: Date of the party:  January 13

1 Date the phone was bought: ....
2 His birthday: ....
3 Date of the exam: ....
4 Date of return from holiday: ....
5 New class starts: ....

Remember
When you hear ordinal numbers in dates (*first, second, third, thirteenth, twenty-second,* etc.), you don't have to write them like this. You can just write the number and the month.

Exam Practice Test 1 — Listening Part 4

Questions 16–20

For each question, choose the correct answer.

16 You will hear two friends talking about shopping.
    What did the boy buy yesterday?
    A something to wear
    B something to eat
    C something to read

17 You will hear a teacher talking to a student called Lyn.
    Why didn't Lyn come to school yesterday?
    A She was sick.
    B She was in a competition.
    C She arrived back late from holiday.

18 You will hear a boy talking about surfing.
    How did he learn to surf?
    A by doing a course
    B by watching videos
    C by practising by himself

19 You will hear a girl talking about her day at school.
    Which subject did she like best?
    A geography
    B English
    C biology

20 You will hear two brothers talking about last night.
    Why did they both sleep badly?
    A Their bedroom was hot.
    B There were noises in the street.
    C They were excited about going on holiday.

Advice

16 When you read the possible answers, think of examples of things you can wear, eat and read.

17 Listen for words that have the same meaning. How does Lyn say she wasn't sick?

*19 What's another way of saying **like best**?*

Training Test 1 — Listening Part 5

In this part, you:
- **read**   two lists of information
- **listen**   to a conversation and **match** the two lists of information

VOCABULARY: JOBS

1 Match the jobs with their descriptions.

Example: grows food —————————————————— journalist
1 writes for a newspaper   dentist
2 looks after sick people   engineer
3 tells people what to do at work   mechanic
4 repairs cars   receptionist
5 looks after people's teeth   nurse
6 builds or looks after machines   manager
7 meets people when they first come to an office   *farmer*

2 Listen and choose the best job for each person. Use some of the words from Exercise 1.

🎧 15

Example: Paul .....*farmer*.....
1 Raquel   ....
2 Adriana   ....
3 Adam   ....

VOCABULARY: SPELLING DAYS AND MONTHS

3 Cross out the wrong spelling.

Example: ~~Joon~~ / June

1 March / Martch   7   July / Juli
2 Mai / May   8   Decimber / December
3 Novembre / November   9   Agost / August
4 January / Janury   10 September / Setember
5 Febuary / February   11 Oktober / October
6 April / Avril

> **Remember**
> Always write days and months with capital letters.

👁 *A2 Key* candidates often forget to use capital letters for days of the week and months.

4 Listen and write the correct day.

🎧 16

Example: Jenny's birthday is on .....Wednesday..... .
1 The speaking test is on ....
2 The trip to the zoo is on ....
3 The football match is on ....
4 The concert is on ....
5 The party is on ....

Exam Practice Test 1 — Listening Part 5

Questions 21–25

For each question, choose the correct answer.

You will hear Lucas talking to his mum about the jobs his friends want to do. What job does each friend want to do?

Example:

0   Lucas   F

Friends

21   Tyler

22   Ava

23   Mark

24   Victoria

25   Bobby

Jobs

A   actor

B   coach

C   dentist

D   journalist

E   mechanic

F   pilot

G   receptionist

H   tour guide

Advice

C What do dentists do?

22 How do you know Ava doesn't want to be a sports coach?

23 Does Mark want to do the same job as his dad?

24 When you hear the information about Victoria, why is **actor** the wrong answer?

You now have 6 minutes to write your answers on the answer sheet.

Training Test 1 — Speaking Part 1

In this part, you:
- **speak** to an examiner
- **answer** questions about yourself, including your name, age, school and hobbies

GIVING PERSONAL INFORMATION

1 Listen to Maria talking to her new classmate, Jose. If the statement is right, put a tick (✓). If it is wrong, put a cross (✗).

Example: Maria is living in England. ✓

1 Maria has got a younger brother.
2 Jose comes from England.
3 Jose is living in Spain now.
4 Jose and Maria are the same age.
5 Maria and Jose are both learning English.

TIP It's important to know what happens in Part 1 of the Speaking test. The information below will help you.

UNDERSTANDING THE TASK

2 Put the information below in the correct order. Write 1–8 in the boxes.

a There will be two examiners there.
b Someone will take you to a room where you will do the speaking test.
c This examiner will ask you questions.
d Your partner will go to the room with you.
e You will give the first examiner your mark sheet.
f You will get a mark sheet with your name on it. [1]
g The second examiner will fill in your mark sheet.
h They will say 'hello' and you will sit down.

TIP The examiner will ask you and your partner some questions about yourselves, such as your names, your ages and where you live.

VOCABULARY: TALKING ABOUT YOURSELF

3 Listen to two students, Daniele and Alex, talking about their school day. Cross out the wrong words.

Example: Daniele starts school **before** / ~~after~~ Alex.

1 Alex *has / doesn't have* lunch at school.
2 Alex likes *history / English* best.
3 Daniele likes *maths / sport*.
4 Daniele *has / doesn't have* to do a lot of homework.

4 Now ask and answer the questions with a partner.
- What time do you start school in the morning?
- What time do you finish?
- What's your favourite subject?
- Do you have sports lessons?
- Do you have to do a lot of homework?

5 Listen to a student telling the examiner about his school. If the statement is right, put a tick (✓). If it is wrong, put a cross (✗).

1 Eduardo goes to a big school. ☐
2 Eduardo knows all the students at his school. ☐
3 Eduardo likes his history teacher. ☐
4 Eduardo doesn't like sport. ☐

6 Listen to another student telling the examiner about something she did with her family. Answer the questions.

1 Where did Elvira go with her family? ....
2 How did they travel? ....
3 What did they do? ....

7 Listen to the examiner's questions from Exercises 5 and 6 again. Give your answers.

> **TIP** Say at least three things when you answer the *Tell me something about ...* question.

UNDERSTANDING THE TASK

8 Put the information below in the correct order. Write 1–8 in the boxes.

a The examiner tells the candidates what topic they are going to talk about. ☐
b The examiner asks candidate A to tell them about something. 4
c The examiner asks candidate B two questions. ☐
d The examiner asks candidate B two questions on the new topic. 6
e The examiner tells the candidates they are going to talk about something different. ☐
f The examiner then asks candidate A two questions on the new topic. ☐
g The examiner asks candidate A two questions. 2
h The examiner asks candidate B to tell them about something. ☐

Exam Practice Test 1 — Speaking Part 1

An examiner is talking to two students. Listen to them answering the questions.

Now listen to the examiner and answer the questions.

> **TIP** The first two questions will be the same for both candidates.
>
> Try not to give one-word answers. For example, if you are asked *How old are you?*, you can say *I'm 13 and my birthday was last week.*, instead of just *13*.
>
> Don't worry if you don't understand a question. The examiner will ask again and use different words.
>
> When the examiner says *Please tell me something about ...*, try to give a longer answer. Think of three things that you can say.

Training Test 1 — Speaking Part 2

In this part, you:
- **speak** to your partner
- **answer** questions the examiner asks you

VOCABULARY: PLACES

1 Listen to two students talking about places to go in their town. How do they describe the places in their town?

Example: the cinema — boring and expensive
1. the sports centre — fun
2. the park — exciting
3. the shopping centre — nice
4. the museum — *interesting*

2 Talk to another student about where you like going in your town.

> **TIP** Listen carefully to the questions the examiner asks. If you don't understand, ask the examiner to repeat the question.

UNDERSTANDING THE TASK

3 Put the information below in the correct order. Write 1–11 in the boxes.

a The examiner asks the candidates a question to talk about. ☐
b The examiner gives the candidates some pictures to look at. [1]
c The candidates talk to each other about the pictures. ☐
d The examiner asks each candidate one or more questions about the pictures. ☐
e The examiner takes the pictures away. ☐
f The examiner repeats the question. ☐
g The examiner asks candidate B the same question and candidate B answers. ☐
h The examiner asks one student (candidate B) a question and candidate B answers. [8]
i The examiner asks candidate A the same question and candidate A answers. ☐
j The examiner asks candidate A another question and candidate A answers. ☐
k The examiner asks both candidates which activity or thing they like best. ☐

Exam Practice Test 1   Speaking Part 2

 Listen to two students doing the test.

 Listen to the examiner's questions again and discuss them in pairs.

Do you like these different places in town? Say why or why not.

TIP You and the other candidate speak together about the things in the pictures.

Both of you should ask questions to each other. Give the other candidate time to speak.

Talk about whether you like the things in the pictures. *Why? Why not?* Use questions e.g. *Do you like …?* or *Do you enjoy …?* or *What do you think about …?*

TIP In Part 2, after looking at the pictures, each candidate is asked the same two questions. Don't just give the same answer as the other candidate.

The questions in Part 2 are often about your opinions, e.g. *Do you prefer …?*

Training Test 2 — Reading and Writing Part 1

- How many questions are there in Part 1?
- Which text types are found there?

VOCABULARY: FOCUS ON MEANING

1 Write the words in the correct column. One word can be used twice.

> 2.5 metres   advertisement   click   desk   film
> homework   main course   memory   website   shower
> swim   swimming costume   ticket   uniform   waiter

Pool	School	Cinema	Computer	Café
2.5 metres				

TIP In Part 1, you may have to read notices or messages. These could be about places like a cinema, swimming pool or school. Try to learn words you might find at these places.

2 Now complete the sentences with some of the words from Exercise 1.

Example: Be careful, the water is ......2.5 metres...... deep.

1 Most pupils in the UK have to wear a school ....
2 How much .... do you have on your computer?
3 The .... brought us our drinks.
4 I wish there weren't so many .... before the films at the cinema.
5 .... to follow the link to our website.
6 You must have a .... before you get into the pool.
7 First, I had soup and for the .... I had an omelette.

3 Match the notices or messages a–c with the correct question 1–3. Then choose the correct answer (A, B or C).

Text	Question	Answer
a	………	………
b	………	………
c	………	………

TIP The notices and messages often have words about times, days and dates.

a

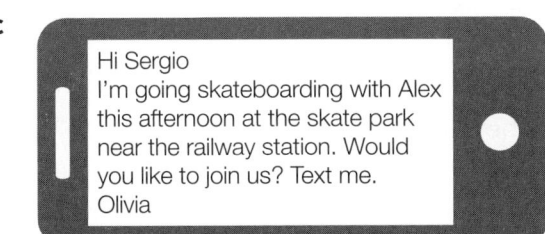

From: Scott
To: Emma

Help! Did you write down the homework for next Wednesday's geography class? I've left my bag at school with the notes in it.

b

School Concert
Buy tickets on the school website, then collect from the office by 1st May.

c

Hi Sergio
I'm going skateboarding with Alex this afternoon at the skate park near the railway station. Would you like to join us? Text me.
Olivia

1 A Pay for tickets before picking them up at school.
    B Keep checking the website to see when the tickets will be available.
    C Let the office know if you need to buy tickets online.

2 What should Sergio do?
    A invite some friends to go skateboarding
    B tell Olivia if he wants to meet her later
    C show Alex where the station is

3 A Scott has forgotten which day the geography class is.
    B Scott wants Emma to help him find his school bag.
    C Scott wants to know what the geography homework is.

Exam Practice Test 2 — Reading and Writing Part 1

Questions 1–6

For each question, choose the correct answer.

1

From 1 October, please do not enter the pool before you have used the shower.

A The pool is closed on October 1st.

B You need to wash before you swim.

C There will be a new shower at the pool.

2

From: Amanda
To: Gran
Subject: Help with a school project

Hi Gran,

Do you have any old photos showing you in your uniform when you were at school? If you do, can you send me one for school?

Thanks,
Amanda

Amanda wants her grandmother to

A let her have a picture.

B lend her some clothes.

C describe her old uniform.

3

Warning

Memory full
Please delete files or click here to buy more memory.

OK

Where might you see this text?

A in a computer shop

B on the screen of a computer

C on the wall in the computer classroom

4

TOMORROW'S TRIP
Time coach leaves school: 8:50.
Please arrive no later than 8:40.
The school gates will open at about 8:30.
Thank you.

What time do pupils need to get to school tomorrow?

A about 8:30

B by 8:40

C at 8:50

5

PLEASE NOTE EVERYBODY
There's a lift if you need it, BUT use the stairs if you can.
It's a great way to stay fit.

A Get the lift if you are in a hurry.

B Use the stairs if the lift is broken.

C Walking up and down stairs is better for you.

6

Hounslow Cinema: Special Offer
Buy tickets to four films and you don't need to pay for the next one!
Every day until 5:30 p.m.

A You can watch up to four films for free.

B The fifth film you see during the daytime is free.

C Cheap tickets are available for groups of four in the evenings.

Advice

1 *What must you do after 1 October?*
2 *What should Gran send to Amanda?*
4 *What does **get to school** mean?*
5 *What's the healthiest way to go up and down in the building?*
6 *Which film is free?*

Training Test 2: Reading and Writing Part 2

- How many texts do you read in Part 2?
- How many questions are there?

VOCABULARY: FOCUS ON MEANING

1 Match words 1–12 with the words in the box which mean the opposite.

| ~~lose~~ | before | start | sad | always | best | large |
| same | enter | love | heavy | nothing | alone | |

Example: win ......*lose*......

1 worst ....
2 everything ....
3 small ....
4 leave ....
5 after ....
6 finish ....
7 light ....
8 happy ....
9 different ....
10 hate ....
11 never ....
12 together ....

GRAMMAR: INFINITIVE WITH *TO* OR *-ING*

2 Cross out the wrong form of the verbs in each sentence.
Example: I want **to go** / ~~going~~ swimming this afternoon.
1 I prefer *studying* / *study* with friends than alone.
2 Lisa hopes *be* / *to be* a doctor one day.
3 Poppy decided *to send* / *sending* an email.
4 The children love *watch* / *watching* cartoons.
5 I enjoy *to read* / *reading* books.
6 I would like *to buy* / *buying* a new phone.

Remember

like / love / enjoy / prefer + verb + *-ing* (going)
want / decide / would like + infinitive with *to* (to go)

GRAMMAR: ADVERBS OF FREQUENCY

3 Match each sentence with an adverb of frequency.

Example: James goes to the park every day. — always

1. Nick goes running every day except Sunday.
2. I play tennis on Mondays, Tuesdays and Fridays.
3. We eat fast food about once a month.
4. Julia doesn't play computer games.

often
sometimes
never
usually
always

4 Now rewrite the sentences from Exercise 3. Use the adverbs of frequency and omit the time expressions in the original sentences.

Example: ..... James always goes to the park. .....

1 ....
2 ....
3 ....
4 ....

TIP You will be presented with, for example, three people, places, books or films, and so on. Make sure you read the text carefully and are not distracted just by the words. Read about each person in turn and see which questions they match.

Reading and Writing Part 2

Training Test 2   49

Exam Practice Test 2 — Reading and Writing Part 2

Questions 7–13

For each question, choose the correct answer.

		Damian	Louis	Jackson
7	Which person says it's better not to look at his phone while he's doing his homework?	A	B	C
8	Which person sometimes does homework with a friend?	A	B	C
9	Which person tells his family when he is working?	A	B	C
10	Which person says that there must be enough light in his room so he can work?	A	B	C
11	Which person thinks that listening to music helps with homework?	A	B	C
12	Which person works in the morning and evening?	A	B	C
13	Which person says it's easier to do homework now than it was before?	A	B	C

Advice

9 Which two people say something about their families? And what's another way to say *tell* someone something?

11 Which person says music helps him work? And who says music doesn't help him?

12 Who works before sleeping and after sleeping?

13 Who says it was difficult to do homework before?

Advice on doing homework

Damian, 13

I don't mind doing homework, especially when I play some jazz (and not pop) on my phone. When I do, I'm able to think more carefully about what I'm doing. Sometimes I really enjoy doing my homework, especially when it's maths and I understand it well. Or when one of my classmates comes to my place and we study together. I find it's best if I let my parents and sister know I'm busy so they don't come into my room and spend all evening talking to me!

Louis, 11

When I started doing my homework in my room every morning, it wasn't a great success. I always found something more interesting to do! But these days, I don't have the same problem. I just go to my room in the evening, switch on the light, sit down at my desk and do it. I do love music, but if I put my MP3 player on, I start to think about the song and not the homework! So I don't listen while I work. It's the same problem if my mum or dad put music on in the next room. I turn my mobile off or put it away before I start. That helps too.

Jackson, 14

I usually do most of my homework before I go to bed. And then I do a bit more as soon as I wake up. I've always found it easy to do that. I'll maybe look at my German vocabulary for five minutes before breakfast. I tell my friends at school: 'If you want to do your homework well, make sure your room is nice and bright. Otherwise, you'll fall asleep!'

Training Test 2 — Reading and Writing Part 3

- What question type is used in Part 3?
- How many questions are there?

VOCABULARY: FOCUS ON MEANING

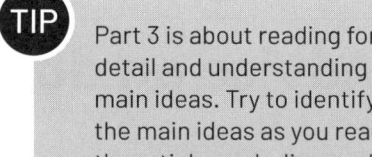

TIP Part 3 is about reading for detail and understanding main ideas. Try to identify the main ideas as you read the article, underline each as you read.

1 Read the text and the questions. For each question, write the number of the line in the text where you found the information needed.

1 The Oakleigh Shopping Centre is opening at last! It took nearly five
2 years to build, but it is now ready! There is a large department store,
3 selling things for the home as well as clothes. There are several
4 smaller shops.

5 You can take a lift to the third floor, where there is a library and a
6 community space for special projects on one floor.

7 We are excited to try Lola's café where you can have a sandwich, or a
8 drink after shopping. There will be 10% discount on all food until the
9 end of the month.

10 You can also save money at the Starway supermarket with its new
11 'shop and save' card. The supermarket has two floors and is one of
12 the largest in the country.

Example: What can you eat at Lola's café?   line ......7......
1 How long did it take to build the shopping centre?   line ....
2 Where is the library?   line ....
3 How much is the discount on food at Lola's café?   line ....
4 When does the discount at Lola's café end?   line ....
5 How can you save money at the supermarket?   line ....

2 Now answer the questions from Exercise 1.
   Example: .....You can eat a sandwich.....

3 Put the phrases in the correct column.

| It's awful   I'm angry about it   It's boring   It's brilliant   I enjoy … -ing   I'm a fan of …
  It's fantastic   It's horrible   I love it   It's pretty   It's terrible   It's the worst |

I like it	I don't like it
	......It's awful......

52 Training Test 2   Reading and Writing Part 3

Exam Practice Test 2 — Reading and Writing Part 3

Questions 14–18

For each question, choose the correct answer.

Starting photography

by Mrs Howells, Class 3D teacher

Have you ever wanted to take better pictures of your family, of your dinner or of your cat? Well, I can help you. In fact, that's what makes photography such a fantastic hobby. It doesn't matter if you have a nice new camera or just use your phone. We photographers are always trying to improve. We want today's photos to be more interesting than yesterday's.

In my photography classes, I'll show you how to find your own style, not just take the same photos as all your friends. But you'll need to be out of bed early and take pictures in the best light, before it gets too bright. We'll talk more about light in Week 1.

Actually, I've never read a book about photography, and I get bored watching videos on the net. I started to understand more about photography by looking at my own photos. I thought about what was wrong with them and decided how to do better next time. And in Week 2, I'll ask you to do the same with photos you have taken.

Do you want to know what I think? I don't think there's anyone who can't take amazing photos. Not everyone wants to, and that's cool. But if you do, come along to Room 4D on Wednesdays after lunch from 1:30 to 2:00.

---

14 Why does Mrs Howells enjoy photography?
- A She loves using her new camera.
- B She likes taking photos of her family.
- C She enjoys trying to take better pictures.

15 What advice does Mrs Howells give?
- A Take pictures with your friends.
- B Don't take photos if it is dark.
- C Take photos early in the morning.

16 How did Mrs Howells learn about photography?
- A from books
- B from her mistakes
- C from videos on the web

17 Mrs Howells believes that
- A everybody should learn photography.
- B photography is a great hobby for everyone.
- C everybody can take good photos if they want to.

18 Why has Mrs Howells written this text?
- A to ask pupils what they like photographing
- B to tell pupils about a photography course
- C to answer pupils' questions about photography

Advice

14 When Mr Howells says *that's what makes photography such a fantastic hobby*, what does that mean?

18 What does this sentence mean: *I don't think there's anyone who can't take amazing photos.*?

Training Test 2 — Reading and Writing Part 4

- How many gaps are there in the text in Part 4?
- How many possible answers are there?

VOCABULARY: *MAKE* AND *DO*

1 Put the words and phrases in the correct columns.

> a cake   a cup of tea   an exam   friends   a good job
> your homework   a mistake   money   a plan   sports
> the washing-up   well

Make	Do
a cake	

2 Now complete the sentences with some of the phrases from Exercise 1.

Example: I have a Saturday job so I can make .....money..... for my holidays.

1 If you make ...., rub it out and start again.
2 I like to do .... with my friends in the park.
3 I'm going to make .... for my mum's birthday.
4 After the course, we have to do ....
5 I usually make my dad .... when he comes home.

VOCABULARY: FOCUS ON MEANING

3 Choose the best word for each space.

1 Maisie is a very good student. She spends a lot of time on her .... She never misses school and she always gets good marks.
   A grades   B studies   C classes

2 In the future, I want to be an engineer. I have an important exam ...., so I don't have time to go to the party.
   A yesterday   B next   C tomorrow

3 Chen comes from China. He lives in Manchester now, but he sometimes .... with his friend in London.
   A stays   B waits   C rests

TIP: In Part 4, think about the meaning of each of the words in A, B and C, and then read the sentence. There is only one possible answer, so think which one works.

Exam Practice Test 2 — Reading and Writing Part 4

Questions 19–24

For each question, choose the correct answer.

The oldest university in the world

Some people say University of Al Quaraouiyine in Morocco is the world's oldest university because there has been a school in the same place **(19)** .... the year 859 AD. In other words, there has been one there **(20)** .... almost 1,100 years. The University has had many famous international students **(21)** .... the years including the great traveller, Ibn Khadun. The University was started by a woman, Fatima al-Fihri and **(22)** .... a long history of teaching women and activities for women's education. Lecturer Hisham Mahmoud believes this helps female students concentrate during their studies. Before joining Al Quaraouiyine, Dr Mahmoud was a scientist, but he decided to **(23)** .... his career and work in education. The University's students all do well. After finishing at the University, many students will continue their **(24)** .... at universities in America and Europe.

19	A since	B between	C after
20	A since	B during	C for
21	A under	B over	C until
22	A has	B makes	C goes
23	A give	B change	C take
24	A marks	B studies	C information

Advice

19 Which preposition is often used with present perfect to talk about a period of time?

23 Dr Mahmoud isn't a scientist now. How could you say that he has a different job?

24 Which word (A, B or C) means 'learning at university or college'?

Training Test 2 Reading and Writing Part 5

- How many gaps are there in the text in Part 5?
- Do you choose a word or think of your own word?

TIP In Part 5, you need to write a word for each gap. Do not just use the first word you think of. Consider if there is a better alternative.

GRAMMAR: COMMON EXPRESSIONS

1 Complete the sentences with words from the box.

| ~~in~~ | ever | go | at | on | too |

Example: He planned to work ….in…. the evening.

1. They met in the park ………… lunchtime.
2. They decided to ………… by train.
3. She arrived at the cinema ………… late and missed the film.
4. It is the biggest peach he has ………… seen.
5. Tomorrow we want to go ………… a trip.

2 Cross out the wrong word in each sentence.

Example: The school is in the centre *of* / ~~in~~ the town.

1. I just got *back* / *returned* from the trip.
2. There are *lot* / *lots* of animals in the zoo.
3. Have *you* / *anyone* seen my phone?
4. Alain has broken *the* / *his* leg.
5. We should take *a* / *an* umbrella.
6. They had a great time *on* / *at* holiday.

GRAMMAR: *BE*, *DO* AND *HAVE*

3 Complete the sentences with the correct forms of *be*, *do* or *have*.

Example: Which film ….did….. you see last night?

1. ……………… you ever been to America?
2. Where ……………… you going?
3. Ricki ……………… not like chocolate.
4. I ……………… meeting Ella this evening.
5. Sophie ……………… met the Queen.
6. What ……………… you do yesterday afternoon?

Remember

Be, *do* and *have* are the auxiliary (helping) verbs. You use *do* for the present and past simple tenses, *be* for continuous tenses and *have* for perfect tenses.

Exam Practice Test 2 — Reading and Writing Part 5

Questions 25–30

For each question write the correct answer.
Write **ONE** word for each gap.

Example: | **0** | WENT |

A school trip to the theatre

Last week, everyone in my class **(0)** .... on a trip to the theatre. We travelled there **(25)** .... coach. The theatre is about 10 kilometres away from school, so it was much **(26)** .... far to walk. The play was *Romeo and Juliet* by William Shakespeare. In fact, it's probably the **(27)** .... famous of all the plays that Shakespeare wrote. We've studied it at school, so I knew **(28)** .... it's about. It's a love story, but it's also the saddest play I **(29)** .... ever seen. At the end, several **(30)** .... the people in my class were crying. But I loved it!

Advice

25 *Which preposition can you use with kinds of transport, e.g. ...... car; ...... train; ...... plane?*

26 *Why didn't they walk to the theatre?*

27 *What tense of **see** can you form with **seen**? What other word do you need to make this tense?*

Training Test 2 — Reading and Writing Part 6

- How many pieces of information must you write in Part 6?
- Do you have to write a story or an email?

TIP Always read the email or instructions carefully and identify the three points you have to write about.

VOCABULARY: FOCUS ON MEANING

1 Read the messages. For each message, choose the best header.

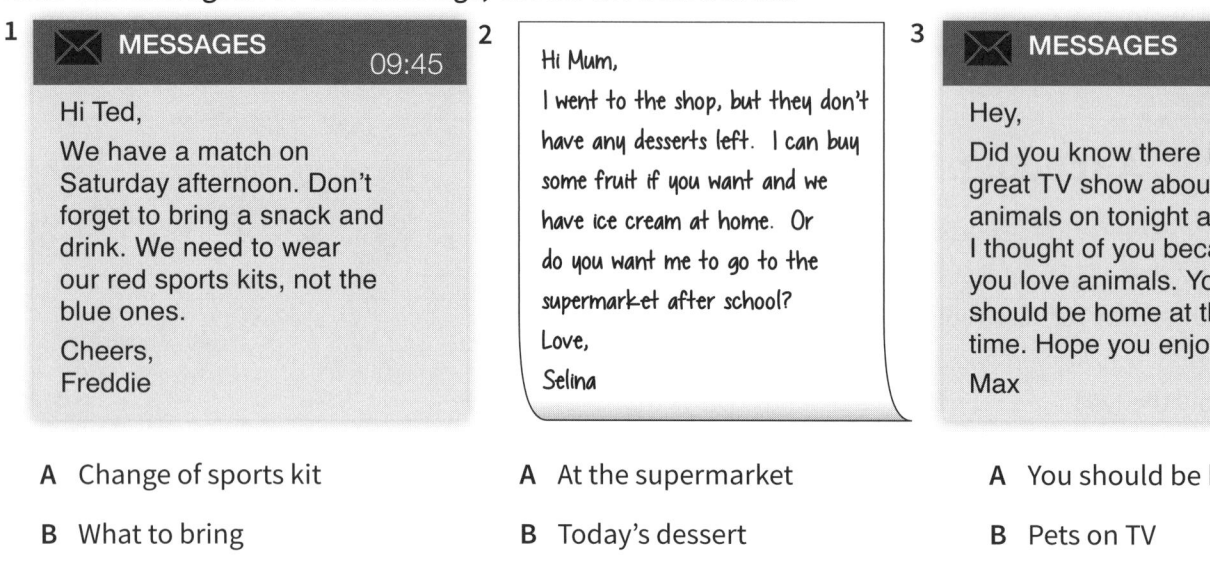

1
- A Change of sports kit
- B What to bring
- C Saturday's match

2
- A At the supermarket
- B Today's dessert
- C I went to the shop

3
- A You should be home
- B Pets on TV
- C TV show tonight

2 Complete the email with the correct words.

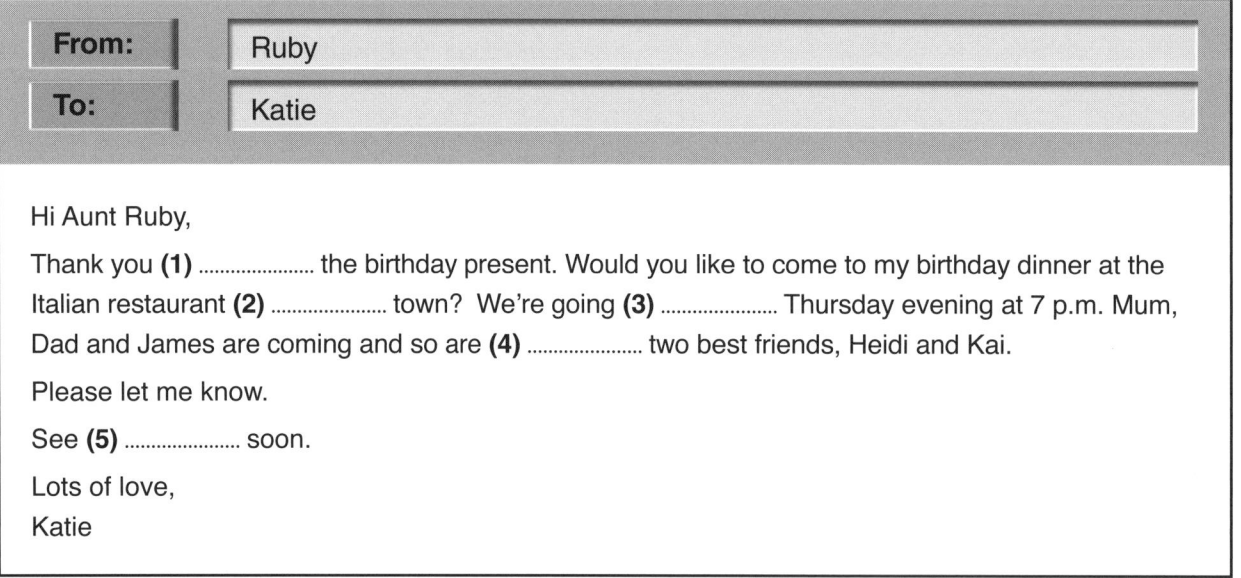

From: Ruby
To: Katie

Hi Aunt Ruby,

Thank you (1) .... the birthday present. Would you like to come to my birthday dinner at the Italian restaurant (2) .... town? We're going (3) .... Thursday evening at 7 p.m. Mum, Dad and James are coming and so are (4) .... two best friends, Heidi and Kai.

Please let me know.

See (5) .... soon.

Lots of love,
Katie

3 Now write sentences for a similar email. Use the questions to help you.

a Where do you want to meet? ....
b What time do you want to meet? ....
c Who do you want to go with you? ....

GRAMMAR: QUESTION WORDS

4 Complete the email with question words from the box.

~~How~~   Where   What   When   Which   Who   Why

From: Saskia
To: Amelia

Hi Amelia,

(0) ...How... are you doing? (1) .... haven't you written to me for so long? I have been very busy lately. (2) .... are you doing at school these days? (3) .... did you go for your school trip this year? We went to the water park.

(4) .... are you sitting next to in your classes this year? I sit next to Lily in English and maths and Pippa in science.

(5) .... can you come to stay? August is the best as we have school holidays. (6) .... week is best for you?

Write soon!
Saskia

Exam Practice Test 2 — Reading and Writing Part 6

Question 31

Read the email from your English friend Sam.

From: Sam
To: Help! I'm bored!

Hi,
I want to ask you something. I'm really bored. Can I borrow something to read from you? What do you think I will enjoy? And when would you like it back?
I hope that's OK. Cheers!
Sam

Advice

It's a good idea to use different words from the words in the question. Try to think of other things to say, so that you don't need to use these words:

borrow > ....

enjoy > ....

like it back > ....

Write an email to Sam and answer the questions.

Write **25 words** or more.

Write the email on your answer sheet.

Training Test 2 — Reading and Writing Part 7

- How many pictures will you see in Part 7?
- Do you write a story or a letter?

GRAMMAR: PUNCTUATION

1 Rewrite the sentences with the correct punctuation.

Example: Come here he said   ....'Come here!' he said....

1. Are you ready yet Gina asked   ....
2. I'm going swimming now said the boy   ....
3. Be quiet shouted the teacher   ....
4. I've never been on a plane before said Jack   ....
5. Where did you put my new pen asked Mrs Green   ....
6. Hurry up please said Abigail   ....

TIP You can use direct speech in your story. Remember to use speech marks (' ') and a comma (,), question mark (?) or exclamation mark (!) after the words the speaker uses.

GRAMMAR: FORM OF TENSES

2 Look at the pictures. Use the words below to make sentences about them.

Louisa   asleep   alarm   rang

ran   school   late   worried

arrived   closed   phone   Saturday   weekend

Example: ....Louisa was in bed....

3 Read the story about the pictures in Exercise 2. Underline five mistakes with the verb forms and tenses. Then correct them.

> Louisa <u>were</u> in bed. She was asleep. Her alarm ringed. She didn't heard it. Louisa woked up late. She running to school. School was closed. She look at her phone. It was Saturday!

Remember
To make simple past sentences negative use *did* + *not* + *verb* (infinitive), e.g. *I didn't wake up.* If the verb is *be*, just add *not*, e.g. *He was not* (*wasn't*) *angry.*

Example: ......was......

1. ....   4. ....
2. ....   5. ....
3. ....

Remember
When you want to join two words like *did* + *not*, the apostrophe (') goes in the place of the letter you cut, e.g. *did not* → *didn't*, *was not* → *wasn't*.

4 Rewrite the sentences using the negative forms.

Example: Anne swam in the sea.   Anne didn't swim in the sea.
1 Tom looked after his little brother.
2 We ate a lot of salad in the summer.
3 I was hungry.
4 Zoe went to school by bus.
5 They took lots of photographs.
6 The children were happy.

> **TIP**
> Time phrases like *in the afternoon, after breakfast* and *at half past five* can make your story more interesting. Words like *then* and *next* help the reader understand when things happen in the story.

GRAMMAR: TIME EXPRESSIONS

5 Read the story. Underline five words or phrases which tell us when something happened.

Last summer, Celia and Eddie went on a special picnic with their mum. In the morning, they made their favourite food and put it in a picnic box. Then they rode their bicycles to the woods. At 12 o'clock, they ate their picnic under the trees. After lunch, the children swam in the lake, while Mum read a book.

6 Now write five sentences about a picnic using time phrases and *after that, next* and *then*.

Exam Practice Test 2 — Reading and Writing Part 7

Question 32

Look at the three pictures.
Write the story shown in the pictures.
Write **35 words** or more.

Write the story on your answer sheet.

> **Advice**
> *Choose a name for the girl in your story.*
> *Describe how she felt before the race. And how did she feel when she won?*
> *Remember to check your work carefully.*

Training Test 2 — Listening Part 1

- How many questions are there in Part 1?
- Do you choose from pictures or written answers?

VOCABULARY: FOOD AND DRINK

1 Read the sentences and unscramble the underlined words.

Example: My favourite drink is apple <u>ujeic</u>.   ....juice....

1. Would you like some <u>rmeca</u> on your hot chocolate? ....
2. In England, we love to eat fish and <u>scpih</u>. ....
3. A lot of people eat <u>oatst</u> for breakfast. ....
4. In summer, we often go for <u>sipnicc</u>. ....
5. Do you put <u>rsuag</u> in your tea? ....
6. You need eggs to make an <u>teemoelt</u>. ....

2 What are they going to eat at the barbecue? Listen and choose the correct answer.

A

B

C

VOCABULARY: FREE-TIME ACTIVITIES

3 Which picture do these words and phrases describe? Write *A*, *B* or *C*.

Example: singing ......C......

1. playing with toys ....
2. taking photographs ....
3. camping ....
4. watching TV ....
5. drawing ....
6. skating ....
7. eating ....
8. dancing ....

A

B

C

4 Look at the pictures in Exercise 3 again. If you can see the object, put a tick (✓). If you can't, put a cross (✗).

Example: camera ✓

1	armchair ☐	6	pizza ☐	12	beach ☐
2	tent ☐	7	phone ☐	13	sweater ☐
3	guitar ☐	8	lake ☐	14	glasses ☐
4	tie ☐	9	television ☐	15	curtain ☐
5	violin ☐	10	sofa ☐	16	sandwich ☐
		11	dress ☐	17	paint ☐

5 Which picture from Exercise 3 is the boy describing? Listen and choose the correct answer.

🎧 29

6 Listen and match people with their phones. Write *A–E*.

🎧 30

Example: Teresa's …B…
1 Dad's ……………
2 Mario's ……………
3 Mum's ……………
4 Leah's ……………

GRAMMAR: NEGATIVE FORMS

7 The sentences below all have a grammar mistake. Underline the words which are wrong. Then write the sentence correctly.

Example: We <u>not</u> see the film yesterday. ……We didn't see the film yesterday.……

1 Alfie will not to go to the party tonight. ………………………………………………
2 Sarah did not born in Spain. ………………………………………………
3 I am not like the cold weather. ………………………………………………
4 The boys are not at the lake last week. ………………………………………………
5 We was not drink juice this morning. ………………………………………………
6 Kathy don't play tennis. ………………………………………………

8 Listen and tick (✓) the sentences you hear.

🎧 31

Example: **A** I can swim. ☐
 B I can't swim. ✓

1 **A** I can't help him. ☐
 B I couldn't help him. ☐
2 **A** We will be home at 6. ☐
 B We won't be home at 6. ☐
3 **A** She doesn't live in London. ☐
 B She didn't live in London. ☐
4 **A** It was raining. ☐
 B It wasn't raining. ☐
5 **A** I haven't any money with me. ☐
 B I haven't got any money with me. ☐

Exam Practice Test 2 — Listening Part 1

 Questions 1–5

For each question, choose the correct answer.

1 What are they going to have for lunch?

A

B

C

2 Which family are Emily's new neighbours?

A

B

C

3 What was Oscar doing when Isabel phoned him?

A

B

C

4 Why didn't Niesha go to the party?

A

B

C

5 Where's Oliver's phone now?

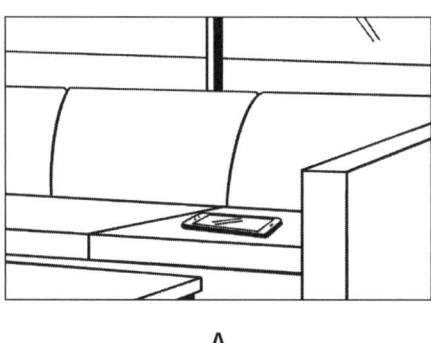
A

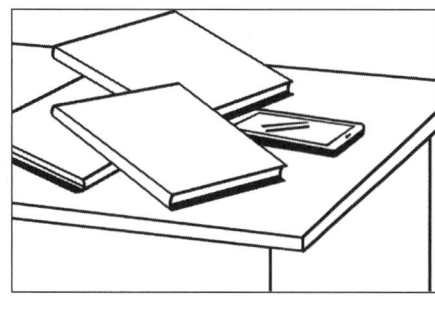
B

C

Advice

1 *If you are not sure about an answer, wait until you hear the recording a second time.*

2 *Look at the pictures carefully! Which family members can you see?*

4 *When a question begins with **Why**, listen carefully for **because** in the text.*

Training Test 2 — Listening Part 2

- Do you listen to one or two people talking in Part 2?
- Do you have to write words or choose answers?

VOCABULARY: ANIMALS

1 Write the words in the correct column.

| ~~duck~~ cat bear elephant fish sheep dog lion chicken rabbit cow tiger camel horse |

Wild animals	Pets	Farm animals
		duck

2 Listen and complete the notes about Ana's pet.

Example: Its name: ......Benji......

1 Its colour: ....
2 Its favourite food: ....
3 It sleeps: in a ....
4 Ana's pet is a ....

VOCABULARY: OPINIONS

3 Cross out the wrong adjective in each sentence.

Example: I love cats. They are so **clever** / ~~noisy~~.

1 Goldfish have *slow / terrible* memories.
2 To work with animals, you must be very *funny / kind*.
3 It is *strange / kind* to keep a bear as a pet.
4 Sheep are *angry / boring*. They don't do anything.
5 Ducks are *amazing / terrible* swimmers.
6 Are tigers as *slow / brave* as lions?

Remember
Some words have a positive or negative meaning so you know what the speaker thinks even if he or she doesn't say *I like ...* or *I don't like ...* .

4 Listen and complete the notes about the zoo.

Example: Boy's favourite animal today: ......horses......

1 Time camel rides end: ....
2 Time zoo opens: ....
3 Time horse rides start: ....

TIP
In Part 2, you often need to listen for places, names, phone numbers or times. Read the notes carefully before you listen so you know what to listen for.

Exam Practice Test 2 — Listening Part 2

Questions 6-10

For each question, write the correct answer in the gap. Write **one word** or **a number** or **a date** or **a time**.

You will hear a woman telling some students about their visit to the zoo.

	Zoo visit
Name of project:	Helping
Animal to draw:	(6) ....
Time to give animals water:	(7) .... a.m.
Name of baby lion:	(8) ....
Age of oldest dolphin:	(9) ....
Get free:	(10) ....

Advice

7 and 9 *Always write times, ages, etc. in numbers, not in words. It's easier!*

10 *Listen carefully for what the students can buy and what they can get for free.*

Training Test 2 — Listening Part 3

- How many questions do you have to answer in Part 3?
- Do you have to write words or circle the answer?

VOCABULARY: WEATHER

1 Match the weather symbols below with the expressions from the box.

| It's sunny. | It's windy. | There's rain. | There's snow. | It's cloudy. | It's foggy. | There's a thunderstorm. |

Example: It's windy.

1 ....
2 ....
3 ....
4 ....
5 ....
6 ....

2 What will the weather be like on Sunday? Listen and choose the correct answer.

🎧 36

A cloudy and foggy   B cold and snowing   C cloudy and windy

VOCABULARY: DESCRIBING PLACES

3 Tick (✓) the words you can use to describe a town or city.

Example: interesting ✓

1	dirty		5	excited		9	thin		13	kind	
2	careful		6	awful		10	friendly		14	important	
3	good-looking		7	lovely		11	expensive		15	broken	
4	boring		8	poor		12	noisy				

UNDERSTANDING CONVERSATIONS

4 Listen to a girl called Ellie telling a friend about her holiday. Read the questions and answers. If the answer is right, put a tick (✓). If it is wrong, put a cross (✗).

🎧 37

Example: Which country did Ellie go to?	Colombia	✗	
1 Who did Ellie visit?	her friend		
2 What is the capital of Sri Lanka?	Colombo		
3 Did they spend long in Colombo?	Yes, they did.		
4 Where is Kandy?	by the sea		
5 What do they grow in Kandy?	tea		
6 What was the weather like?	very hot		
7 How long was the second flight?	4 hours		
8 What did Ellie bring back?	coffee		

TIP If you are not sure of an answer in any part of the test, choose or write an answer anyway.

Exam Practice Test 2 — Listening Part 3

Questions 11–15

For each question, choose the correct answer.

You will hear Jasmine talking to her aunt about a camping trip.

11 Where did Jasmine and her aunt go swimming?
   A in the sea
   B in the river
   C in the lake

12 How did Jasmine feel about sleeping in a tent to start with?
   A excited
   B afraid
   C unhappy

13 What did Jasmine's aunt like cooking?
   A omelette
   B steak
   C pasta

14 Jasmine's aunt thought the campsite
   A needed a shop.
   B had good showers.
   C was too small.

15 Which activity did Jasmine like best?
   A cycling
   B fishing
   C running

Advice

11 Remember that when you say *too ... to do something* (e.g. too windy to swim in the sea), it means you couldn't do it.

12 How did Jasmine feel about sleeping in a tent after the first night?

14 When you say *It's a pity*, are you happy or unhappy about something?

Training Test 2 — Listening Part 4

- How many questions do you have to answer in Part 4?
- Do you have to write words or circle the answer?

VOCABULARY: PLANS AND INTENTIONS

1 Read the conversation. What kind of words go in the gaps? Then listen and complete the conversation.

Rosa: What are you **(0)** ...doing... at the weekend?

Abdullah: My team is **(1)** .... on Saturday. I'm **(2)** .... my cousins and going with them. After that, we might eat out. What about you?

Rosa: I'm **(3)** .... in on Saturday. I've got lots of homework. But on Sunday I'm **(4)** .... a film with my family.

Abdullah: That's nice. I'm **(5)** .... my grandparents on Sunday.

2 Listen and choose the correct answer.

The woman

A wants a sandwich.   B is going to eat some fruit.   C is going to have lunch.

GRAMMAR: COMPARATIVE ADJECTIVES

3 Write sentences about Steve and Dan using the adjectives from the box.

~~tall~~	long	fat
slim	young	old
strong	short	weak

Example: .....Steve is taller than Dan.....

Steve   Dan

4 Who is younger than Luke? Listen and choose the correct answer.

A Sally   B Simon   C David

MAIN IDEA

5 Listen to Penny talking about her family. Tick (✓) the main idea.

a Her sister needs help getting dressed. ....
b She does the shopping for her mum. ....
c Being the oldest child is hard. ....
d She helps her brother with his homework. ....

TIP In some Part 4 questions, you need to listen for the most important idea or the topic. Listen carefully and think about everything you hear. What does the speaker really want to say?

6 What are Patsy and Michael talking about? Listen and choose the correct answer.

A Anna's party last night   B a football match   C why they are at the doctor's

Exam Practice Test 2 — Listening Part 4

 Questions 16–20

For each question, choose the correct answer.

---

16 You will hear a girl, Teresa, talking to her friend.
Who's Teresa waiting for?
- A a classmate
- B a member of her family
- C a teacher

17 You will hear a boy phoning his mother.
Why is he phoning her?
- A to ask about something
- B to give her some news
- C to say sorry for something

18 You will hear two friends talking about a new café.
How will they find out where the new café is?
- A They'll ask another friend.
- B They'll check on the internet.
- C They'll look at a poster.

19 You hear a girl and her dad talking about a boat tour.
Why do they decide to go on the boat tour today?
- A It's cheap today.
- B The weather's good.
- C They know the guide.

20 You will hear a boy, Hugo, talking to his teacher.
What must Hugo do first?
- A help another teacher
- B help the school secretary
- C help another student

Advice

16 *Remember that some words can have different meanings. What different meanings has the word* **coach** *got?*

18 *Listen carefully! The possible answers are not usually in the same order as the information in the recording.*

20 *Remember that* **Thank you. But actually ...** *is a nice way of saying no.*

Training Test 2 — Listening Part 5

- Do you listen to one person speaking or a conversation in Part 5?
- Do you have to match words or circle the answer?

VOCABULARY: HOBBIES

1 Write the words in the correct column.

| chef | keyboard | brush | music | act | cooker | lake | costumes | sea | colours |
| concert | artist | kitchen | bake | a play | sail | theatre | paints | piano | boat |

Acting	Playing the piano	Sailing	Painting	Cooking
				chef

2 Listen. Match the speakers with their hobby.

1 Amanda   swimming
2 James   drawing
3 Marion   walking
                     sailing
                     acting

> **TIP** In the second list, the words you hear are often different to the words you read. Other words which you hear will help you choose the correct answer. For example, you might not hear **swimming**, but you may hear **pool**.

3 Listen again and write the words that helped you choose your answers.

SAYING THINGS IN DIFFERENT WAYS

4 Match the phrases with similar meanings.

Example: a show of the art — an exhibition of the pictures

1 has been to Italy, France, Spain and Germany   plays in a band
2 movies that make you laugh   takes lots of pictures
3 his cakes are amazing   visited different countries
4 is in a rock group   funny films
5 enjoys photography   he's good at baking

> **TIP** There are different ways to say the same thing. Knowing different phrases with similar meanings can help you in the Listening test.

Exam Practice Test 2 — Listening Part 5

Questions 21–25
46 For each question, choose the correct answer.

You will hear a girl talking to her mum about her friends and their hobbies. What hobby does each friend have?

Example:

0   Mateo   H

Friends

21   Hannah
22   Christopher
23   Samantha
24   Andrew
25   Grace

Hobbies

A   acting
B   being in a band
C   building models
D   climbing
E   learning languages
F   photography
G   swimming
H   watching movies

Advice

B *What's another way of saying* band*?*

E *Which two languages do you hear about in the recording?*

23 *Who has Samantha's model planes now?*

You now have 6 minutes to write your answers on the answer sheet.

Training Test 2 — Speaking Part 1

- How many students will there be in the room when you do your speaking test?
- How many examiners will there be?
- Who will you speak to in Part 1?

TALKING ABOUT FREE TIME

1 Match the questions and answers.

Example: What do you enjoy doing in your free time?

1 Where do you spend your free time?
2 Who do you spend your free time with?
3 When do you have most free time?

I have a lot of free time at the weekend.
I usually spend my free time at home.
I usually spend my free time with my friends.
I enjoy listening to music and playing games.

TIP Remember to give more information than one-word answers.

2 Now ask and answer the questions with a partner.

ASKING FOR REPETITION

3 Listen to a student talking to the examiner. Answer the questions.
1 What does the student say when she doesn't understand?
   a What?
   b Sorry?
2 Which word is not a polite way to ask someone to repeat something?

4 Listen to two students talking to an examiner. How many questions does the boy ask the examiner to repeat?

Remember
After you've answered some questions, one of you will have to tell the examiner about something.

TIP If you don't understand something, ask the examiner to repeat it.

5 Listen again and tick (✓) the phrases the boy uses.

Could you say that again, please? ☐
Could you repeat that? ☐
I'm sorry, what did you say? ☐
I don't understand. ☐
Sorry? ☐

TIP If you want the examiner to repeat something, please ask politely.

Exam Practice Test 2 — Speaking Part 1

🎧 49 An examiner is talking to two students. Listen to them answering the questions.

🎧 50 Listen to the examiner and answer the questions.

TIP
Remember that you only need to answer the questions. You don't need to ask questions to the examiner or the other candidate.

In Part 1 phase 2, both candidates are asked different questions.

When you answer a question, try to add more information.

Training Test 2 — Speaking Part 2

- Who do you speak to in Part 2?
- Who will ask you questions?
- What will you look at with your partner?

TALKING ABOUT SPORT

1 Listen to two friends talking about sports they like and don't like. How do they describe the sports?

Example: football — dangerous
1 swimming — popular
2 volleyball — boring
3 cycling — exciting
4 running — difficult

2 How many questions will the examiner ask you after they take the pictures away? Will the examiner ask you the same questions?

3 Listen to two students talking to an examiner about sport. What did the examiner ask Carlos and Monika when they just gave a one or two-word answer?

4 Complete the answers so they are true for you.

1 Do you prefer doing sports with friends or alone?
   I prefer doing sports *with friends / alone* because ....

2 Do you like watching sport on television?
   I *like / don't like* watching sport on television because ....

3 Is there a sport you would like to try?
   I'd like to try .... because ....

4 Do you like taking part in sports competitions?
   I *like / don't like* taking part in sports competitions because ....

TIP Try to explain your answers in this part of the test.

Exam Practice Test 2 — Speaking Part 2

Listen to two students doing the test.

Listen to the examiner's question again and in pairs discuss them.

Do you like these different sports? Say why or why not.

TIP

Find out what your partner thinks. Say if you agree or don't agree with them.

Remember to look at the other candidate while you are speaking to them.

Remember to give reasons for your answers, e.g. *I think football is fun to watch **because it is exciting**.*

If you need time to think of an answer, you can say *That's an interesting question ...* while you decide what to say.

Test 3 Reading and Writing Part 1

Questions 1–6

For each question, choose the correct answer.

1

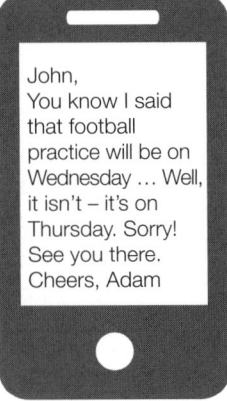

John,
You know I said that football practice will be on Wednesday ... Well, it isn't – it's on Thursday. Sorry! See you there.
Cheers, Adam

Why has Adam written this message?

A to ask if John wants to play football

B to tell John that Adam can't play football

C to let John know about a change of plan

2

SCHOOL FESTIVAL OF BOOKS

Meet Ralph Sparks.
Hear how he got ideas for his books, including *History of Exploring the New World*.
Thurs 9 a.m. Room D31.

Pupils can

A buy books.

B read about explorers.

C come and listen to a writer.

3

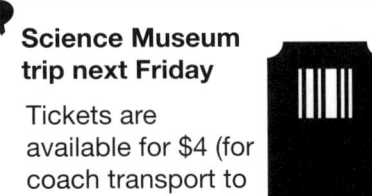

Science Museum trip next Friday

Tickets are available for $4 (for coach transport to the museum, and for museum entry).
If you're interested, see Mr Goss.

A You can now buy tickets for the museum trip.

B Tell Mr Goss how you want to travel to the museum.

C Mr Goss will tell you if you need a ticket to the museum.

4

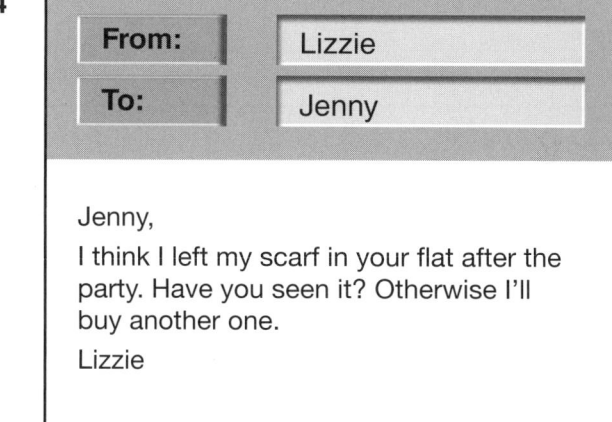

From: Lizzie
To: Jenny

Jenny,
I think I left my scarf in your flat after the party. Have you seen it? Otherwise I'll buy another one.
Lizzie

Why has Lizzie written this?

A to invite Jenny to a party

B to tell Jenny about a shopping trip

C to ask about something that she's lost

5

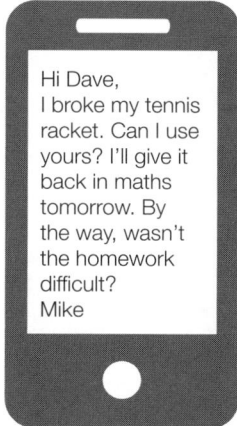

Hi Dave,
I broke my tennis racket. Can I use yours? I'll give it back in maths tomorrow. By the way, wasn't the homework difficult?
Mike

Mike wants to

A play tennis with Dave.

B borrow something from Dave.

C get help from Dave with the homework.

6

Mr Gregson is away today. Class 3, at 9 a.m., please go and join Class 4 in Room 7C for geography. Mr Gregson will be back tomorrow.

A There isn't a geography lesson tomorrow.

B Class 4's lesson is happening at a different time today.

C There will be more people in Room 7C than usual today.

Test 3 — Reading and Writing Part 2

Questions 7–13

For each question, choose the correct answer.

		Gaurika Singh	Tracy Austin	Nadia Comăneci
7	Which sports person now works as a journalist?	A	B	C
8	Which sports person made her sport more popular?	A	B	C
9	Which sports person won something that she couldn't use?	A	B	C
10	Which sports person became rich when she was young?	A	B	C
11	Which sports person was the youngest person in a competition?	A	B	C
12	Which sports person did something that people believed was not possible?	A	B	C
13	Which sports person was born in one country and now lives in another?	A	B	C

Three teenage sports superstars

Gaurika Singh, swimmer

Gaurika is from Nepal, and she was the only under-14-year-old to take part in the 2016 Olympics in Rio de Janeiro. She swam the 100 metres backstroke for Nepal. Home for Gaurika these days is in the UK, and she trains at the Copthall Swimming Club, where the coaches have trained other world-class swimmers. Her father, Paras Singh, travels with her around the world when she goes to a competition.

Tracy Austin, tennis player

When Tracy Austin was given a car as a prize in a tennis competition in Stuttgart, Germany, she was 15 and still too young to drive, but she was already a professional tennis player. Then, at the age of 17, the American became the youngest ever sports person to earn a million dollars. Before long, she was the world's number one player. These days, she often appears on TV, talking about tennis matches at major competitions.

Nadia Comăneci, gymnast

When Romanian gymnast Nadia took part in the Olympic Games in Montreal, Canada, in 1976, she immediately became one of the most famous sports people in the world. She got perfect scores of 10.0 in seven different events. Everyone thought that nobody could do this and, in fact, 9.9 was the highest number that the score board could show. She did so well that she helped large numbers of people become interested in gymnastics.

Test 3 Reading and Writing Part 3

Questions 14–18

For each question, choose the correct answer.

Lots of people become good at something when they are young. And quite a lot of children know what career they want to follow when they are older. But not everyone opens their own company. This is exactly what Isabella Rose Taylor has done. She started designing clothes when she was eight years old.

At the time, she was a keen painter. She used a lot of reds, blues and yellows, and these colours helped her to think of new clothes which she could make.

When she started designing and making clothes, Isabella just made clothes for fun. But people liked her designs, so soon she started selling them online. Now she has a business and takes part in fashion shows. She runs her business from the family home, where she has made one room into an office, and another into a studio where the clothes are made.

Isabella has also found time to finish school and get a college degree. She's intelligent, and she has thousands of followers online who love her stuff. It's brilliant that she already has people who work for her. Above all, she really knows what is needed to succeed in the world of fashion. And I am sure that she will.

'The way I see it is I get to follow my dream and be a teenager at the same time. I think I'm pretty lucky,' she says.

14 What does the writer say is unusual about Isabella Rose Taylor?
  A She planned her future career when she was very young.
  B She started her own business when she was very young.
  C She got interested in fashion when she was very young.

15 What does Isabella say about painting and making clothes?
  A It is important to paint good pictures of clothes.
  B The colours in her paintings gave her ideas for clothes to make.
  C She uses paint to put her favourite colours on the clothes she makes.

16 What do we learn about Isabella's home?
  A Everything for her business is done in the same room at home.
  B Her home is too small, so she's looking for another one.
  C She's made changes to her home so that she can work there.

17 Why does the writer think that Isabella will do well in the future?
  A She is already very popular online.
  B She understands the fashion business.
  C She has brilliant people who work for her.

18 What is the best title for the article?
  A The girl who can't wait to start working in fashion soon
  B The problem with working and studying
  C A hobby that is becoming a career

Test 3 Reading and Writing Part 4

Questions 19–24

For each question, choose the correct answer.

Ferry to School

Most pupils go to school each day on foot or by car, but Jordan Basford is different. He lives on the Scottish island of Egilsay. There, the school had to (19) .... because there weren't any other pupils. The nearest school is in Rousay, across the sea. His family have a boat, but it is small, and they can (20) .... use it in good weather. A much larger boat is (21) .... in bad weather. So every day, Jordan has to (22) .... the ferry across the sea to go to school. He usually comes back home afterwards, but sometimes he phones home to say that he's (23) .... the night at a friend's house instead. 'I know I have to travel a long (24) .... to school each day,' he says. 'But I don't mind.'

19 A close   B complete   C finish

20 A almost   B only   C nearly

21 A needed   B liked   C had

22 A travel   B make   C catch

23 A resting   B staying   C sleeping

24 A way   B transport   C mile

Test 3 — Reading and Writing Part 5

Questions 25–30

For each question, write the correct answer.
Write **ONE** word for each gap.

Example: 0 | THE

From: Jake
To:

Hi guys!

This is (0) .... best holiday ever! Plakias is such (25) .... beautiful place. The meals in the hotel are fantastic. For breakfast, you can have as (26) .... as you want. I usually have yoghurt with lots of fruit. There's lots for everyone in my family (27) .... do, so we're all enjoying it. Tomorrow I'm going to try windsurfing (28) .... the first time. I'm really excited because I (29) .... never done it before, but Dad says it's easy. In fact, I love it here so much that I (30) .... like to come back next year!

See you soon.

Jake

Test 3 — Reading and Writing Part 6

Question 31

You are planning a party. Write an email to your English friend Malcolm.
In your email:

- **tell** Malcolm about your party
- **ask** if Malcolm wants to come
- **suggest** what Malcolm should bring.

Write **25 words** or more.
Write the email on your answer sheet.

Test 3 Reading and Writing Part 7

Question 32

Look at the three pictures.
Write the story shown in the pictures.
Write **35 words** or more.

Write the story on your answer sheet.

Test 3 — Listening Part 1

Questions 1–5

For each question, choose the correct answer.

1   What time does the nature programme start?

A

B

C

2   Who is Diana talking to on her mobile?

A

B

C

3   Where will Henry put his mum's watch?

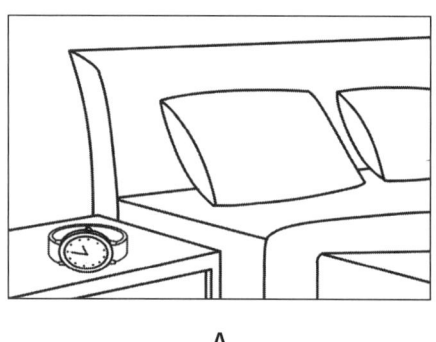
A

B

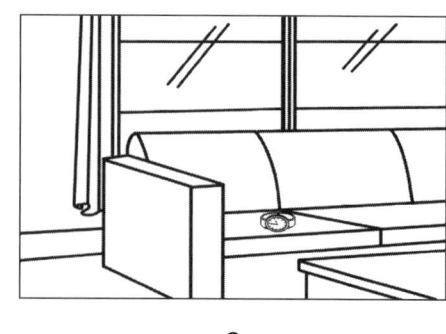
C

4 Why is the girl tired?

A

B

C

5 What will the weather be like on Sunday?

A

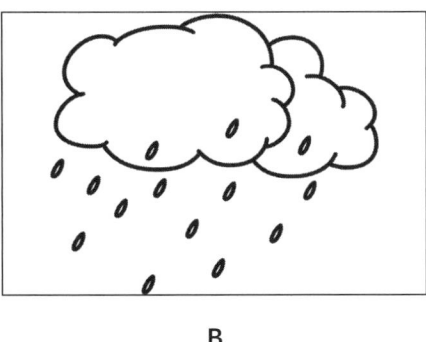

B

C

Test 3 Listening Part 2

 Questions 6–10

For each question, write the correct answer in the gap. Write **one word** or **a number** or **a date** or **a time**.

You will hear a boy leaving a message for a friend about a football match.

Football match

Day:	Saturday
Name of stadium:	(6) ....
Bus number:	(7) ....
Cost of ticket:	(8) £ ....
Wear:	(9) ....
Bring:	(10) ....

Test 3 Listening Part 3

Questions 11–15

For each question, choose the correct answer.

You will hear Hitomi talking to her friend Freddie about her visit to Hardin Castle.

11 Who did Hitomi go to Hardin Castle with?
   A   her classmates
   B   her family
   C   her neighbours

12 What was the weather like?
   A   cold
   B   wet
   C   windy

13 What do Hitomi and Freddie both like best at Hardin Castle?
   A   the Queen's bathroom
   B   the yellow bedroom
   C   the dining room

14 Freddie went to the castle because he wanted
   A   to learn about history.
   B   to take photos.
   C   to find out about birds.

15 What's on at the castle next month?
   A   a running race
   B   an exhibition of old cars
   C   a painting course

Test 3 Listening Part 4

 Questions 16–20

For each question, choose the correct answer.

16 You will hear a girl talking about a video.
Which part of the video didn't she understand?
 A the beginning
 B the middle
 C the end

17 You will hear two friends talking about a concert.
What's the boy's opinion of the concert?
 A It was boring.
 B It was terrible.
 C It was unusual.

18 You will hear a boy talking to his dad about going to the city centre.
Why are they going to the city centre?
 A to meet someone
 B to buy something
 C to watch something

19 You will hear a teacher talking to his class.
What information is he giving his students?
 A They're going to start a new project.
 B They're going to have their lesson outside.
 C They're going to have a longer lesson.

20 You will hear a boy talking about his sister, Emma.
Who has Emma married?
 A an artist
 B a tour guide
 C a cook

Test 3 Listening Part 5

Questions 21–25

For each question, choose the correct answer.

You will hear Angela talking to her uncle about the problems with her old school. What problem was there in each place in the school?

Example:

0   hall   F

Places		Problems
21 cafeteria	☐	A crowded
22 library	☐	B noisy
23 classrooms	☐	C not clean
24 lift	☐	D not modern
25 office	☐	E not useful
		F too far
		G too small
		H too warm

You now have 6 minutes to write your answers on the answer sheet.

Test 4 Reading and Writing Part 1

Questions 1–6

For each question, choose the correct answer.

1

A There is 30% off all tickets.

B You can save money this week.

C Tickets are only available this week.

2 We can only take you on the school trip if your parents have said it's OK. Please ask them to fill in the form.

A Parents can come on the trip if they want.

B Pupils must fill in a form and show it to their parents.

C The school can take pupils on the trip if their parents let them go.

3

The school's sports hall is used by all pupils for gym and indoor sports. There is also an outdoor area for hockey and football.

This text is

A describing the sports lessons at the school.

B explaining where you can do sports at the school.

C saying that the pupils at the school are good at sports.

4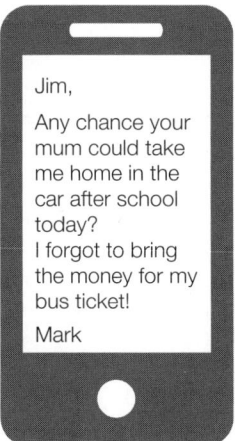

What does Mark want to do?

A borrow some money

B travel home with Jim

C invite Jim to visit him

5

Who can join the singing group?

A anyone at the school

B pupils who have music lessons

C people who can already read music

6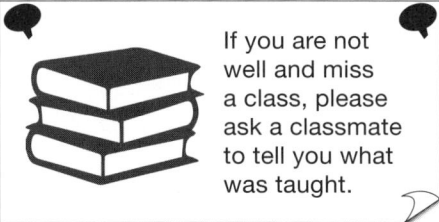

Who is this message for?

A pupils who are feeling ill

B pupils who couldn't go to a lesson

C pupils who would like to help their friends

Test 4 Reading and Writing Part 2

Questions 7–13

For each question, choose the correct answer.

		My First Cookbook	Cooking for Students	Everybody Can Cook
7	Which book won a prize?	A	B	C
8	Which book has healthy recipes?	A	B	C
9	Which book shows that cooking can be fun?	A	B	C
10	Which book has dishes from different countries?	A	B	C
11	Which book teaches words to talk about food?	A	B	C
12	Which book is about food that the writer's family liked?	A	B	C
13	Which book has pictures of someone preparing the food?	A	B	C

Cookery books for young people

This week, we look at three books about cooking for young people.

My First Cookbook by Lenard Minnow

Lenard Minnow's last cookery book was a huge success across the world. And now, he has written a cookery book just for children. It has lots of lovely reading activities, so that children can get to know the names of more unusual foods. It explains in an easy-to-read way how to cook and makes it clear that cooking can be a hobby that young and old can really enjoy.

Cooking for Students by Cormac O'Dally

The idea for this book came when Cormac O'Dally's two sons went away to university. They never cooked and had no idea what to do in the kitchen, so Cormac wrote this book to help them. The photo on the cover of the book shows Cormac and his sons laughing and enjoying the food together. Students who use this book won't win prizes for great new food ideas. The meals are very simple, like cheese on toast, but they're easy to prepare and good for you, too.

Everybody Can Cook by Denise Macon

With its 'look-as-you-cook' photos, you can see the author doing everything that you need to do in this wonderful new book. And, as the title says, you'll soon be able to make tasty meals. Many of them come from all four corners of the world. The author received £4,000 when the book was chosen as *Cookbook of the Year* in a competition this year.

Test 4 Reading and Writing Part 3

Questions 14–18

For each question, choose the correct answer.

An amazing stay at the Ocean View Hotel

I'm usually sad to say goodbye to my cousins after visiting them in Australia. But last June I wasn't. We had to change planes in the Middle East on the way back and had to stay overnight. I just couldn't wait to get to our hotel.

The first thing I noticed in the hotel was all the glass. It was really bright, so I don't know why all the lights were on in the building! There was also loud rock music playing, which I loved (but my parents didn't)! There weren't many people waiting at the reception, so we were soon in our rooms.

The garden wasn't what I expected. 'Dad,' I said, 'you told me there was a pool!' He took me back into the reception area and then up in the lift to the 39th floor and out onto the top of the building. 'Here it is,' he said. It was amazing! Swimming under the clouds was awesome.

I've stayed in some great hotels around the world, but nothing as cool as that one! I saw photographs of it before I went, but they don't really show how large the building is. I couldn't believe it. Everything is huge – the building, the pool, the meals (which were delicious, too, by the way)! There's so much to do and see there. I hope we can go back again and stay for longer!

14 The writer says that last June, she felt
   A excited about where she was going.
   B sad because she was leaving her cousins.
   C angry because of the delay in her journey.

15 What was the hotel like inside?
   A dark
   B noisy
   C busy

16 Where was the hotel's pool?
   A in the hotel garden
   B on the roof of the hotel
   C close to the hotel's reception area

17 What do we learn about the writer in the last paragraph?
   A She hasn't visited many hotels in her life.
   B She didn't have time to see everything in the hotel.
   C She didn't know the hotel is so big.

18 Why has the writer written this text?
   A to describe what the hotel looks like
   B to say how the hotel could improve
   C to explain why she loved the hotel

Test 4 Reading and Writing Part 4

Questions 19–24

For each question, choose the correct answer.

The Museum of Childhood

The Museum of Childhood in Edinburgh is full of variety. Visitors can (19) .... dolls houses, toy cars and much more. There is everything from toy soldiers to board (20) .... The museum was started by a man called Patrick Murray, who (21) .... many toys during his life and wanted to show them to the public. But it's more than (22) .... a museum of toys. It explores all parts of growing (23) ...., and its exhibitions include lots of different things, from storybooks to baby (24) .... The museum is easy to find in the centre of Edinburgh and is open all year.

19 A watch   B look   C see

20 A games   B competitions C matches

21 A picked   B collected   C took

22 A already   B just   C yet

23 A up   B out   C away

24 A snack   B food   C meal

Test 4 — Reading and Writing Part 5

Questions 25–30

For each question, write the correct answer.
Write **ONE** word for each gap.

Example: 0 — TO

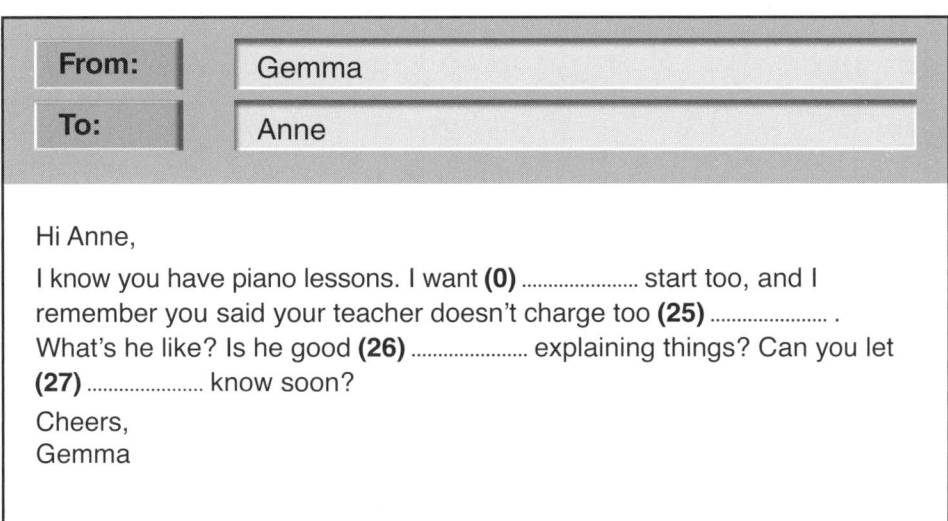

From: Gemma
To: Anne

Hi Anne,

I know you have piano lessons. I want **(0)** .... start too, and I remember you said your teacher doesn't charge too **(25)** .... What's he like? Is he good **(26)** .... explaining things? Can you let **(27)** .... know soon?

Cheers,
Gemma

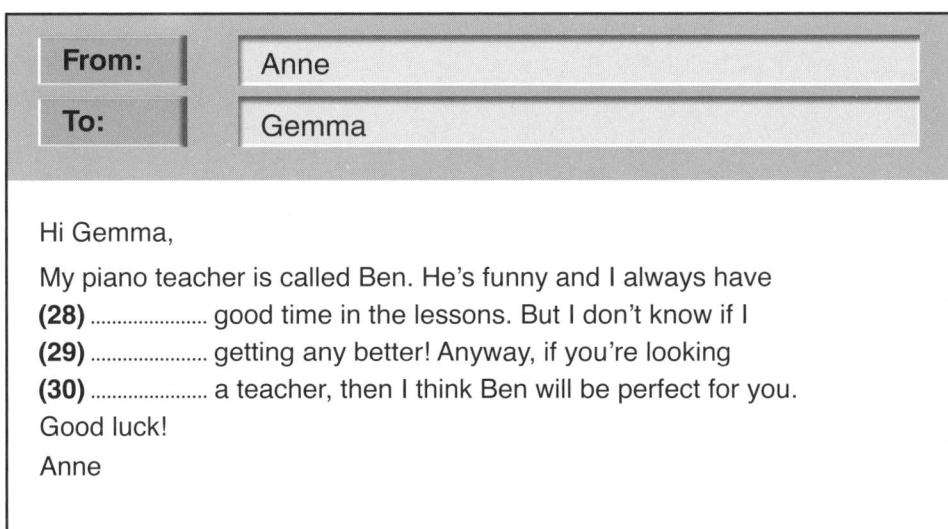

From: Anne
To: Gemma

Hi Gemma,

My piano teacher is called Ben. He's funny and I always have **(28)** .... good time in the lessons. But I don't know if I **(29)** .... getting any better! Anyway, if you're looking **(30)** .... a teacher, then I think Ben will be perfect for you.

Good luck!
Anne

Test 4 Reading and Writing Part 6

Question 31

You recently lost something when you were in town with your English friend Alfie.
Write an email to Alfie.
In your email:

- **say** what you have lost
- **explain** how you think you lost it
- **tell** Alfie what you want him to do to help.

Write **25 words** or more.
Write the email on your answer sheet.

Test 4 — Reading and Writing Part 7

Question 32

Look at the three pictures.
Write the story shown in the pictures.
Write **35 words** or more.

Write the story on your answer sheet.

Test 4 — Listening Part 1

Questions 1–5

For each question, choose the correct answer.

1 How much did the boy's football shirt cost?

£11.75	£20.50	£35.00
A	B	C

2 What did Sophie enjoy doing most at the weekend?

A   B   C

3 Where did Paul stay on holiday this year?

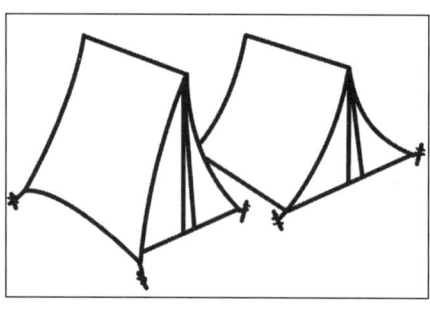  

A   B   C

4 Which subject will they study first today?

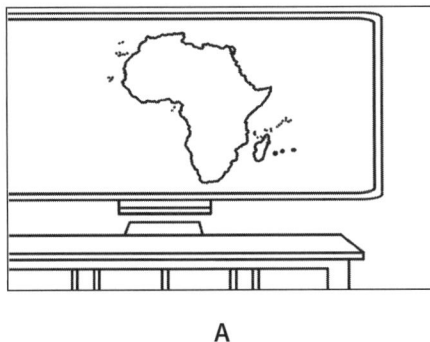

A

B

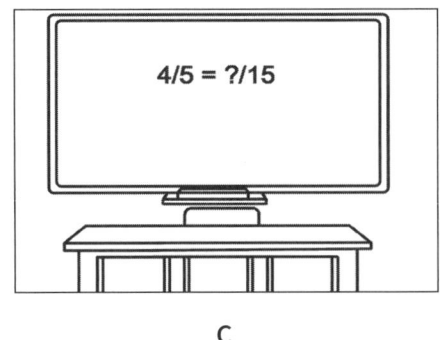

C

5 Why was Tina late for school today?

A

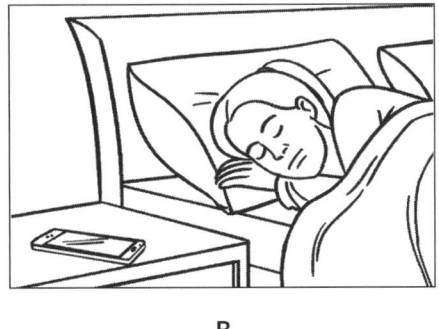

B

C

Test 4 Listening Part 2

Questions 6–10

 For each question, write the correct answer in the gap. Write **one word** or **a number** or **a date** or **a time**.

You will hear Rosie's aunt telling her about a dance competition.

Dance competition

For children from:	13–15
Date to enter by:	(6) ....
Send:	(7) ....
Website address:	(8) www. .... .com
Place:	(9) ....
First prize:	(10) £ ....

Test 4 Listening Part 3

 Questions 11–15

For each question, choose the correct answer.

You will hear Tommy talking to his friend Olga about their class party.

11 Which date is the class party?
   A   25th June
   B   28th June
   C   1st July

12 What does Olga think Tommy should wear to the party?
   A   his black jeans
   B   his blue shorts
   C   his green T-shirt

13 What's Olga worried about?
   A   singing at the party
   B   playing the guitar
   C   helping tidy up

14 Why will Tommy arrive at the party late?
   A   He'll have to wait for a lift.
   B   There aren't many buses.
   C   He wants to play tennis first.

15 What's Olga going to take to the party?
   A   some balloons
   B   some paper plates
   C   some food

Test 4 Listening Part 4

 Questions 16–20

For each question, choose the correct answer.

16 You will hear two classmates talking together.
   How did the girl come to school today?
   A by car
   B by train
   C on foot

17 You will hear a girl talking to a man who works at a museum.
   What's the girl looking for?
   A her bag
   B her coat
   C her folder

18 You will hear a boy talking about learning French.
   How did he improve his French?
   A by visiting France
   B by watching French cartoons
   C by emailing his French penpal

19 You will hear a girl talking to her aunt about her hobbies.
   Which hobby does the girl like doing now?
   A looking after animals
   B taking photos of animals
   C collecting toy animals

20 You will hear a headteacher talking to the whole school.
   What's new at the school this year?
   A a cafeteria
   B a sports hall
   C a music room

Test 4 — Listening Part 5

Questions 21–25

For each question, choose the correct answer.

You will hear a boy talking to a friend about the presents he bought during a family trip round Europe. What present did he buy in each country?

Example:

0 Germany E

Countries

21 Poland

22 Switzerland

23 Italy

24 Spain

25 Portugal

Presents

A backpack

B calendar

C dictionary

D guidebook

E kite

F mug

G photo album

H postcards

You now have 6 minutes to write your answers on the answer sheet.

Test 5 Reading and Writing Part 1

Questions 1–6

For each question, choose the correct answer.

1. School singing practice starts this week. Please don't arrive later than 1:25, as we must all be ready by 1:30.
    Thank you.

    A Singing practice starts at 1:25.

    B There is no singing practice this week.

    C Please arrive early for singing practice.

2.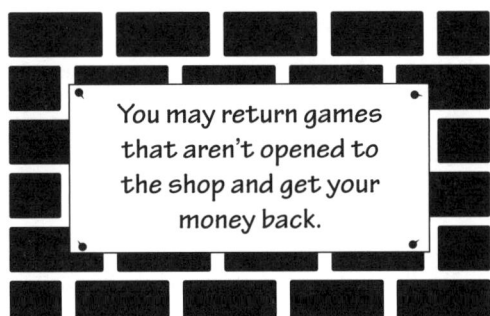
    You may return games that aren't opened to the shop and get your money back.

    You can return a game if

    A it doesn't work.

    B you don't like it.

    C you haven't used it.

3.
    Book club
    Do you enjoy discussing books with classmates? Yes? Then come along to the book club. To join, contact Mr Sponforth.

    Speak to Mr Sponforth if

    A you are interested in becoming a member of the book club.

    B you would like to borrow a book from the club.

    C you have read the same book as your classmates.

4

Hi Dad! It's Sam's birthday, so I want to buy a present. Could you lend me enough to get him something from the bookshop? Thanks! Davey

Davey wants to

A go shopping with his dad.

B borrow some money.

C ask what to get for Sam.

5

HONEY CAFÉ
Unfortunately two of our staff are ill today. (We must have at least three to open.) Open at 9 a.m. tomorrow.

A The café is closed today.

B We are looking for more staff.

C Tomorrow we open at a different time.

6

Smitford's Computer Store
Bring us your old laptop* when you get a new one from us and receive **£100** off.
*must still work

A We repair old laptops.

B Old laptops are for sale for £100.

C Save money when you buy a new laptop.

Reading and Writing Part 1

Test 5   111

Test 5 — Reading and Writing Part 2

Questions 7–13

For each question, choose the correct answer.

		Noa Mintz	Mikaila Ulmer	Jessie Chong
7	Which person is helping wildlife?	A	B	C
8	Which person has given someone a job?	A	B	C
9	Which person gets ideas for her business from nature?	A	B	C
10	Which person wants to teach children about business?	A	B	C
11	Which person has opened other companies before?	A	B	C
12	Which person is pleased that she took some good advice?	A	B	C
13	Which person thinks she has improved as a business person?	A	B	C

Three teenage business people

Noa Mintz

Noa started a business when she was 8, holding art classes for children. Two years later, she began a party planning business for children. She doesn't think that went very well. She thinks that because she was very young, the business wasn't exactly perfect. These days, she is sure that she knows what she's doing, as she has a business that finds staff to look after other people's children. She also pays someone to help her with the business.

Mikaila Ulmer

Mikaila has opened a company called *Me and the Bees*. It sells lemonade, which is made with local honey. The drink is sold in several shops in Mikaila's home town and online, and some of the money is given to nature groups that work with bees and other insects. Mikaila also shows children and their families how to get ideas to make money. She says, 'I think I've got lots of good advice for them.'

Jessie Chong

When Jessie was really young, her parents told her that she should find something that she loved doing. She's happy she did because she thinks everyone should love their work. Jessie makes jewellery and sells it online. She looks at flowers and plants, and then uses the shapes and colours she sees in her jewellery.

Test 5 Reading and Writing Part 3

Questions 14–18

For each question, choose the correct answer.

Where playing video games IS real life

Seo-yun Cho doesn't have time for hobbies because she spends all her time playing video games. 'I practise as much as I can so I will improve,' she says. 'This is what I really need to do.'

Seo-yun and her friends are members of KS Fireflies 6, a video game team. She and the other members share a flat in Seoul's business district. Since they all left school, they have managed to make playing video games their life.

Every day, Seo-yun gets up after a good night's sleep at 10 a.m. and goes for a jog for an hour, before sitting down at her computer and starting to play. She and her friends have a few breaks to eat and relax during the day and the evening, but Seo-yun thinks that after midnight is when she has more fun playing than at any other time. She usually goes to bed at 3 a.m.

Seo-yun and the rest of the team need to train hard and keep fit, as top players need to do about 500 mouse-clicks a minute. Video games are big business in South Korea, and the best players (like KS Fireflies 6) usually become even better-known than top baseball or volleyball players.

Some people might get bored after playing video games for an hour or two. But these guys are actually getting paid to do something they love as a job. Many of them would even like to do it for free!

14 What is the most important thing for Seo-yun Cho?
   A trying new video games
   B getting better at video games
   C finding enough time to play video games

15 Seo-yun and her friends
   A live together.
   B went to school together.
   C have a business together.

16 What does Seo-yun say about playing games at night?
   A It's when she feels happiest.
   B It's the time that she most enjoys playing.
   C It sometimes makes her tired.

17 What does the writer say about sports?
   A Seo-yun and her friends play a lot of sports video games.
   B Seo-yun and her friends play sports to get fit.
   C Seo-yun and her friends are more famous than some sports players.

18 Why does the writer think that Seo-yun and her friends are lucky?
   A because they earn a lot of money
   B because they don't need to look for another job
   C because they are doing something that they love

Test 5 Reading and Writing Part 4

Questions 19–24

For each question, choose the correct answer.

Preparing to go camping with the school

From choosing the right equipment to remembering to take spare socks, campers need to be prepared! Keen camper, Jody Walterson, 16, explains why.

Most pupils are really excited when they are taken on a school camping **(19)** .... They're becoming really popular these days. For example, my class goes camping at **(20)** .... once a year. It's usually just for one night, but it's sometimes **(21)** ....

Parents and children need to work together to **(22)** .... sure that everything goes well. Part of this is deciding what to take – this is a really important **(23)** .... It's a good idea to take more clothes than you think you will **(24)** .... So, if you're going for two nights, take three pairs of socks. And don't forget your toothbrush or a charger for your phone!

19	**A** way	**B**	journey	**C**	trip
20	**A** little	**B**	least	**C**	low
21	**A** longer	**B**	bigger	**C**	higher
22	**A** get	**B**	do	**C**	make
23	**A** job	**B**	work	**C**	occupation
24	**A** have	**B**	like	**C**	need

Test 5 — Reading and Writing Part 5

Questions 25–30

For each question, write the correct answer.
Write **ONE** word for each gap.

Example: | **0** | ABOUT |

From: Joanna
To: Emma

Hi Emma,

At school, you said that you don't have any plans for the weekend. Well, how **(0)** .... meeting on Saturday morning? I thought maybe we could go **(25)** .... a bike ride. We can go to Moreton-on-Sea, and get something **(26)** .... eat. I went there by bike last year. In fact, there were six **(27)** .... us, and we had **(28)** .... really amazing day. I don't think it will take more **(29)** .... four hours to get there and back. Can you let **(30)** .... know if you can come?

Hopefully, I'll see you then!

Cheers,
Joanna

Test 5 Reading and Writing Part 6

Question 31

Read the email from your English friend Liam.

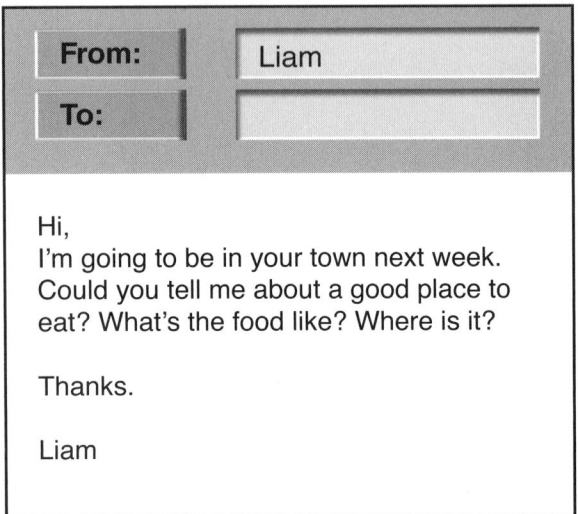

From: Liam
To:

Hi,
I'm going to be in your town next week. Could you tell me about a good place to eat? What's the food like? Where is it?

Thanks.

Liam

Write an email to Liam and answer the questions.
Write **25 words** or more.
Write the email on your answer sheet.

Test 5 — Reading and Writing Part 7

Question 32

Look at the three pictures.
Write the story shown in the pictures.
Write **35 words** or more.

Write the story on your answer sheet.

Test 5 Listening Part 1

 Questions 1–5

For each question, choose the correct answer.

1 How will Luciana invite her friends to her birthday party?

A

B

C

2 What does Charlie want to borrow from his brother, James?

A

B

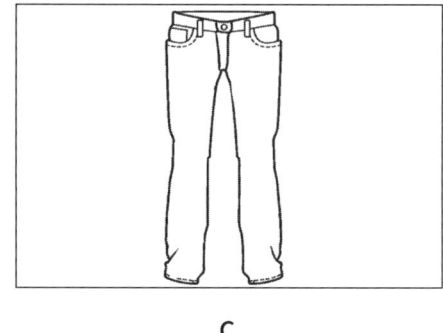
C

3 How will Carol get to her dance class?

A

B

C

4 Which film do they decide to watch first?

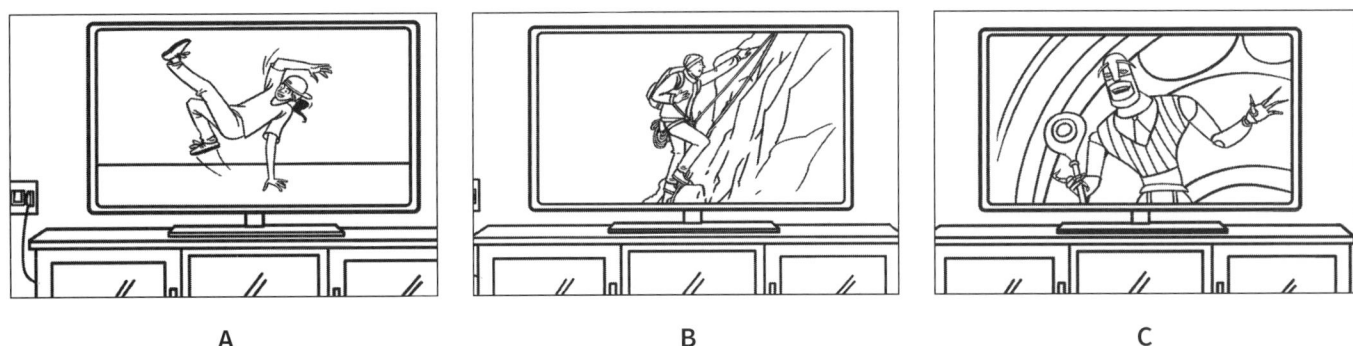

A   B   C

5 Which T-shirt does the girl like best?

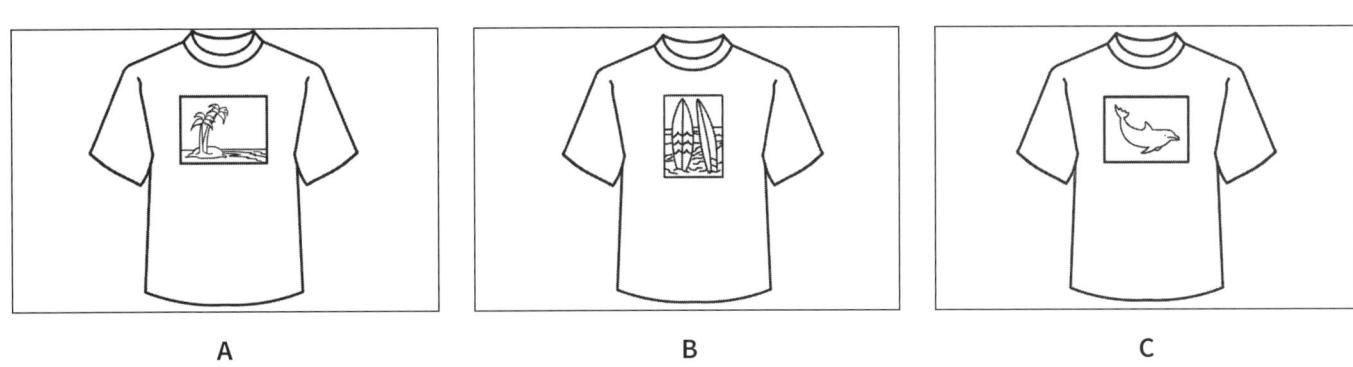

A   B   C

Test 5 — Listening Part 2

 Questions 6–10

For each question, write the correct answer in the gap. Write **one word** or **a number** or **a date** or **a time**.

You will hear a boy leaving a message for a friend about some homework.

Homework

Subject:	English
What to write:	(6) ....
Number of words:	(7) ....
Remember to add:	(8) ....
Get ideas from:	(9) www. .... .com
Date to give to teacher:	(10) ....

Test 5 Listening Part 3

Questions 11–15

For each question, choose the correct answer.

You will hear Dan talking to a shop assistant in a sports shop.

11 Dan thinks plastic skateboards are
   A cheap.
   B popular.
   C light.

12 What colour skateboard does Dan prefer?
   A purple
   B yellow
   C grey

13 The shop assistant says the best skateboard for Dan is about
   A 16 cm wide.
   B 18 cm wide.
   C 20 cm wide.

14 What free gift can Dan get from the shop?
   A a backpack
   B some gloves
   C a scarf

15 When will Dan buy a skateboard?
   A on Wednesday
   B on Friday
   C on Saturday

Test 5 Listening Part 4

Questions 16–20

For each question, choose the correct answer.

16 You will hear two friends talking about eating healthy food.
Why are they talking about eating healthy food?
  A They've just read about it.
  B They've just watched a video about it.
  C They've just listened to a talk about it.

17 You will hear a boy talking about his history project.
Who gave him some information about it?
  A a person who works as a guide
  B a woman who lives near him
  C a teacher he knows

18 You will hear a girl talking about her clothes.
Why does she want to buy some new clothes?
  A to look nice at a party
  B to go on holiday
  C to play a new sport

19 You will hear a teacher talking about a problem.
Where is there a problem?
  A in the playground
  B in the sports hall
  C in the cafeteria

20 You will hear a brother and sister talking about their pet rabbit.
What don't they like about having pets?
  A talking to them
  B brushing them
  C giving them food

Test 5 Listening Part 5

Questions 21–25

For each question, choose the correct answer.

You will hear a boy talking to a classmate about the things he is going to do next week. What is he going to do on each day?

Example:

0 Monday $\boxed{C}$

Days

21 Tuesday ☐

22 weekend ☐

23 Wednesday ☐

24 Thursday ☐

25 Friday ☐

Things to do

A finish a school project

B go on a trip

C go to a party

D help a neighbour

E make a meal

F send emails

G take money to school

H visit the city library

You now have 6 minutes to write your answers on the answer sheet.

Test 6 Reading and Writing Part 1

Questions 1–6

For each question, choose the correct answer.

1

Please don't eat ice creams here. They aren't good for our books! Please finish them outside before you come in. Thanks.

Where might you see this?

A in a café

B in a library

C in a picnic area

2

FOUND
One school bag
Inside: one key and a phone

Contact Mrs Thompson if you think it might be yours.

Speak to Mrs Thompson if

A you've got an extra key.

B you have lost something.

C you know where the bag is.

3

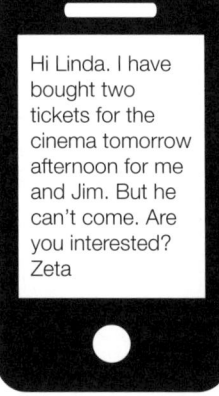

Hi Linda. I have bought two tickets for the cinema tomorrow afternoon for me and Jim. But he can't come. Are you interested? Zeta

Zeta has written to

A invite Linda to go and see a film.

B ask Linda what films she's interested in.

C tell Linda where to meet Jim tomorrow.

4

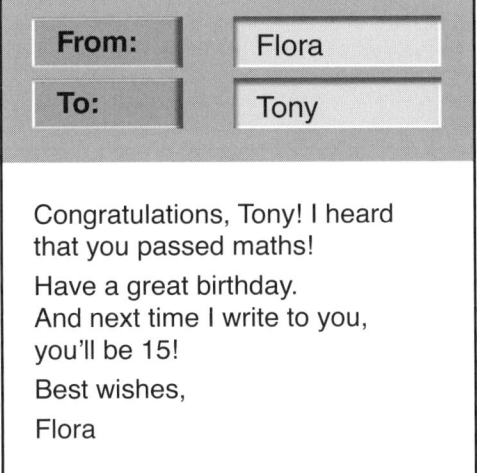

What has Tony just done?

A met Flora

B had a birthday

C done well in an exam

5

NO EXIT
The door isn't working correctly. Use door opposite to get to the science room.

A Please go to the science room now.

B You can't go out through this door.

C The science laboratory is being used by other people today.

6

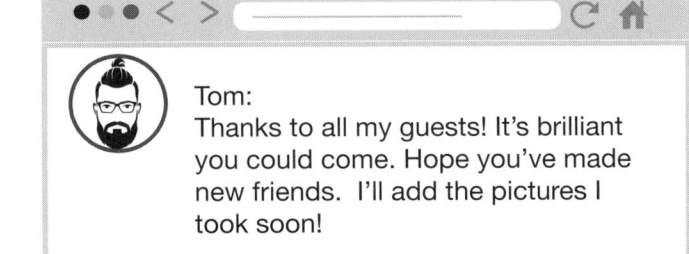

Tom:
Thanks to all my guests! It's brilliant you could come. Hope you've made new friends. I'll add the pictures I took soon!

Tom is writing about

A a party that he had.

B a picture that he saw.

C some people that he has just met.

Test 6 Reading and Writing Part 2

Questions 7–13

For each question, choose the correct answer.

		Melissa	Sharon	Latifa
7	Which person has made new friends because of her hobby?	A	B	C
8	Which person does her hobby near her home?	A	B	C
9	Which person says she is getting better at her hobby?	A	B	C
10	Which person does her hobby with a family member?	A	B	C
11	Which person wants to do her hobby more often?	A	B	C
12	Which person needs to buy something for her hobby?	A	B	C
13	Which person says her hobby was more expensive than she thought?	A	B	C

Three teenagers describe their hobbies

Melissa, runner

I started running about a year ago. At first, I just ran 1 or 2 kilometres, but I now do about 10. My speed is improving too. I've joined a running club in the town centre. I didn't know any of the members before, but now most of them are my mates. My dad was a keen runner when he was younger – he was really fit, but he stopped when he hurt his leg. Actually, I need to order some new running shoes – just a simple pair. I don't think the expensive ones make you run faster!

Sharon, skateboarder

I go skateboarding most evenings in the park. I suppose that's quite a lot, but the park is only a minute or two from our apartment, and I only stay there half an hour or so. Although I stay longer when my friends are there. Sometimes my cousin's there too. He's a beginner, and I'm teaching him a few moves. He's starting to get really good!

Latifa, rock climber

Two of my best friends suggested I should start rock climbing, so now the three of us do it together. The mother of one of them takes us once or twice a month, but I'd like to do it every week. When I started, I didn't know you need to get so much stuff – and it isn't exactly cheap! I really love it. I don't think I'll ever get bored of climbing!

Test 6 — Reading and Writing Part 3

Questions 14–18

For each question, choose the correct answer.

Would you like to be an astronaut?

You don't have to be Superman to fly in space. Many men and women from many different countries have done it. For example, the European Space Agency (ESA) now has 14 astronauts from 8 different countries.

The first thing is this – you need to be sure it's the job that you really want to do. It requires a lot of hard work and several years of study at university before astronaut training even begins. Most people start this between 27 and 37 years of age. Many astronauts also train to become pilots first.

Astronauts come from all over Europe and the world, and it's important that they can speak the same languages. They have to speak English, and they are given Russian lessons. Some also learn another language, for example Japanese, as a number of astronauts are Japanese speakers.

If you are still at school and you'd like to be an astronaut when you're older, it's not too early to start developing the skills you will need. Playing video games is a great thing to do, as it helps you to think quickly and clearly. This is what you will need to do when you travel in space.

Another good thing to do is sports, especially team sports. They make you fit, of course, but more importantly, they help you learn how to do things together with your colleagues. So, maybe planning a game of football for next weekend isn't a bad idea?

14 The first paragraph says that
  A lots of people can be an astronaut.
  B there are astronauts from all countries.
  C only 14 people from Europe have become astronauts.

15 The writer says
  A you need to be a pilot before you become an astronaut.
  B it's important to know that being an astronaut is right for you.
  C when you start training to be an astronaut, you must be between 27 and 37.

16 Which languages do ESA astronauts know how to speak after training?
  A English and Russian
  B English and Japanese
  C English, Japanese and Russian

17 Why can playing video games be useful if you want to be an astronaut?
  A There are many video games about space travel.
  B Video games can teach you to think fast.
  C Video games help you to understand how computers work.

18 How can sports help you to become an astronaut?
  A They help you to get fit.
  B They give you something to do in your free time.
  C They help you to work well with other people.

Test 6 — Reading and Writing Part 4

Questions 19–24

For each question, choose the correct answer.

Cello player wins music competition

A 17-year-old musician has won the Young Musician of the Year Prize. Alex Guo was competing (19) .... her brother and four other musicians under the (20) .... of 21 to win the prize. The winner was (21) .... after the young musicians each played on stage with a band. When she (22) .... that she was the winner, she was so excited. 'I just couldn't (23) .... it,' she said. 'Music has always been a (24) ...., but now I want it to be my job, too.'

19	A over	B against	C after
20	A age	B years	C time
21	A taken	B found	C chosen
22	A heard	B listened	C agreed
23	A guess	B believe	C thank
24	A hobby	B fun	C game

Test 6 — Reading and Writing Part 5

Questions 25–30

For each question, write the correct answer.
Write **ONE** word for each gap.

Example: 0 | ARE

From: Mrs Hammond
To: Class 9

Dear Class 9,

Next week, we **(0)** .... going to do something different in our English lesson. I want pupils to stand up, and speak to the whole class for one minute about a sport they like doing. It will be an excellent way **(25)** .... practise your English. If you **(26)** .... like to do this, please **(27)** .... me know.
Mrs Hammond

From: Andrew
To: Mrs Hammond

Dear Mrs Hammond,

Thank you **(28)** .... your email.
My favourite sport is football. I love talking about it, and I can **(29)** .... everybody about the team I play in **(30)** .... Saturday afternoons. I hope that is OK.
Best wishes,
Andrew

Test 6 Reading and Writing Part 6

Question 31

Read the email from your English friend Joe.

Hi,

Sorry, I know I said I can meet you tomorrow afternoon, but I can't. Can we meet next week instead? When are you free? And where is a good place to meet?

Cheers,

Joe

Write an email to Joe and answer the questions.

Write **25 words** or more.

Write the email on your answer sheet.

Test 6 — Reading and Writing Part 7

Question 32

Look at the three pictures.
Write the story shown in the pictures.
Write **35 words** or more.

Write the story on your answer sheet.

Test 6 — Listening Part 1

 Questions 1–5

For each question, choose the correct answer.

1 How did Carrie hurt her leg?

A

B

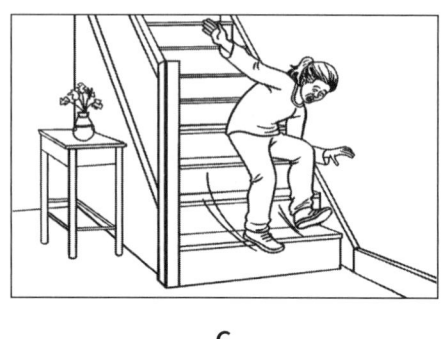

C

2 Which backpack has the boy bought?

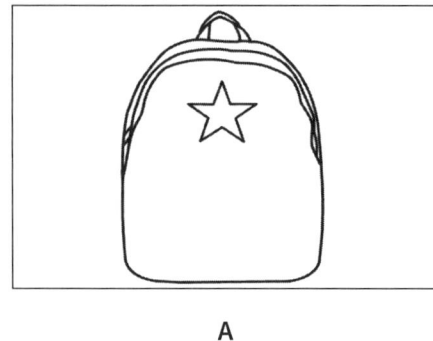

A

B

C

3 Where will Daisy have her birthday party?

A

B

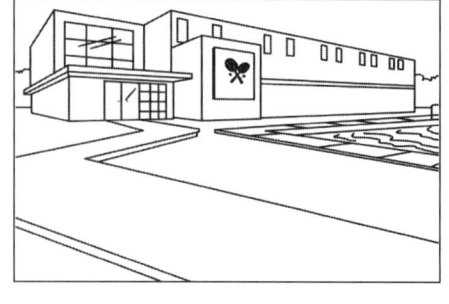

C

4 Which job does Dylan's dad do now?

A

B

C

5 What did they both do yesterday?

A

B

C

Test 6 — Listening Part 2

Questions 6–10

For each question, write the correct answer in the gap. Write **one word** or **a number** or **a date** or **a time**.

You will hear a teacher telling some students about a class trip.

Class trip

Visit a:	castle
Cost of trip:	(6) £ ....
Day of trip:	(7) ....
Time bus leaves school:	(8) .... a.m.
Bring:	(9) ....
Name of special exhibition:	(10) ....

Test 6   Listening Part 3

 Questions 11–15

 For each question, choose the correct answer.

You will hear Nadia and Tom talking about their new school.

11 How will Nadia get to their new school?
- A by bike
- B by bus
- C on foot

12 What doesn't Tom like about the school uniform?
- A the jacket
- B the shirt
- C the trousers

13 How many students are there in the new school?
- A under 500
- B about 800
- C more than 1000

14 Which subject does Nadia like?
- A chemistry
- B maths
- C biology

15 What will they do on the first day?
- A have a class quiz
- B visit the school library
- C meet all their teachers

Test 6 Listening Part 4

Questions 16–20

For each question, choose the correct answer.

16 You will hear a teacher talking about a trip.
   What has changed?
   A   the cost
   B   the time
   C   the transport

17 You will hear two students talking about a problem.
   Where's the boy's phone?
   A   in the teacher's desk
   B   in his brother's bag
   C   in his house

18 You will hear a boy talking about buying some boots.
   Why did he buy the boots?
   A   They're comfortable.
   B   He likes the colour.
   C   They're in fashion.

19 You will hear a girl talking about playing tennis.
   How does she feel after playing?
   A   angry
   B   hungry
   C   tired

20 You will hear two friends talking about a new teacher.
   What do they like about the new teacher?
   A   He's clever.
   B   He's friendly.
   C   He's famous.

Test 6 — Listening Part 5

Questions 21–25

For each question, choose the correct answer.

You will hear a girl talking to her uncle about the books she has read at school. How does she feel about each book?

Example:

0   *The Delay*   H

Books

21   *Crunch*

22   *My Island*

23   *Dangerous Animals*

24   *The Invitation*

25   *Skating Star*

Feelings

A   boring

B   funny

C   good beginning

D   hard to understand

E   sad

F   scary

G   too short

H   useful

You now have 6 minutes to write your answers on the answer sheet.

Speaking Tests 1–6 | Part 1

Greetings and introductions
At the beginning of Part 1, the examiner greets the candidates, asks for their names and where they come from.

Giving information about self
The examiner asks the candidates questions about two topics. They may be asked, for example, to talk about their school, their family, their free time or hobbies, food, the internet, etc.

Extended response
After the examiner has asked questions about a given topic, candidates are expected to give an extended response to a *Now, please tell me something about …* prompt. The topics are of a personal and concrete nature. Candidates should produce at least three utterances in their extended response.

Test 1 | Speaking Part 1

(3–4 minutes)

Phase 1

		Back-up prompts
Examiner *To each candidate in turn*	What's your name, please? How old are you? Where do you come from? Where do you live?	Are you from (Poland)? Do you live in (Gdansk)?

Phase 2

		Back-up prompts
Examiner	Now, let's talk about your day at school.	
	Candidate A, what time do you go to school each day?	Do you go to school early each day?
	What is the first thing you do when you get to school?	Do you go into your classroom when you get to school?
	Candidate B, how many lessons do you have each day?	Do you have six lessons at school every day?
	What time do you finish school?	Do you finish school before 4 o'clock in the afternoon?
		Back-up questions
Extended Response	Now, Candidate A, please tell me something about what you like about your school.	Do you see your friends at school every day? Do you have much free time at school? Can you play sports or games at your school?

		Back-up prompts

Now, let's talk about your families.

Candidate B, how many people are there in your family?

Do you have a large family?

Who is the oldest person in your family?

Is there anyone very old in your family?

Candidate A, where do the people in your family live?

Do the people in your family live in this town?

When will you next see your family?

Will you see your family today?

Back-up questions

Extended Response   Now, Candidate B, please tell me something about how your family spend time together on special occasions.

Do you go somewhere special with your family on birthdays?
Do you eat something together?
Do you often spend time with your family?

Speaking Part 2

(5–6 minutes)

Phase 1 (3–4 minutes)

Examiner   Now, in this part of the test you are going to talk together.
Shows Test 1 visuals (page 43) to both candidates.
Here are some pictures that show different places in a town.
Do you like these different places in town? Say why or why not. I'll say that again.
Do you like these different places in town? Say why or why not.
All right? Now, talk together.

Candidates   ....
Allow a minimum of 1 minute (maximum of 2 minutes) before moving on to the following questions.

Examiner /   Do you think …
Candidates
Use as appropriate.   … cinemas are exciting?
Ask each candidate   … shopping centres are interesting?
at least one   … bus stations are dirty?
question.   … museums are boring?
  … parks are beautiful?

Optional prompts
Why?/Why not?

What do **you** think?

Examiner   So, Candidate A, which of these places in town do you like best?
And you, Candidate B, which of these places in town do you like best?
Thank you. (Can I have the visuals, please?)
Retrieve the visuals.

Phase 2 (Up to 2 minutes)

Examiner   Now, Candidate B, do you prefer going back to the same places in your town or going to lots of different places? (Why?)
And what about you, Candidate A? (Do you prefer going back to the same places in your town or going to lots of different places?) (Why?)
Where do you think is the best place in this town to meet friends, Candidate A? (Why?)
And you, Candidate B? (Where do you think is the best place in this town to meet friends?) (Why?)

Thank you. That is the end of the test.

Test 2 Speaking Part 1

(3–4 minutes)

Phase 1

Examiner	What's your name, please?	**Back-up prompts**
To each candidate in turn	Where do you live?	Do you live in (Madrid)?
	How old are you?	

Phase 2

Examiner Now, let's talk about hobbies.

Back-up prompts

Candidate A, what hobbies do you enjoy doing in your spare time?

Do you enjoy playing sports?

Where do you do your favourite activities?

Do you do some of your hobbies at home?

Candidate B, how often do you do your favourite hobby?

Do you do your favourite activity every week?

What hobbies do other people in your family enjoy?

Do other people in your family enjoy visiting new places?

Back-up questions

Extended Response Now, Candidate A, please tell me something about a hobby that you enjoy doing with friends.

Is playing computer games one of your hobbies?

Do your friends and you enjoy doing the same thing?

Have you always done this hobby with the same people?

Back-up prompts

Now, let's talk about school subjects.

Candidate B, what subjects do you study at school?

Do you study geography and history at school?

When did you start learning English?

Did you start learning English when you were nine?

Candidate A, which foreign languages are you studying at your school?

Are you learning other foreign languages?

How often do you have maths lessons?

Do you have maths lessons every day?

Back-up questions

Extended Response Now, Candidate B, please tell me something about your favourite subject at school.

Is English your favourite subject?

Have you always enjoyed studying this subject?

Do you have a lot of homework with this subject?

Speaking Part 2

(5–6 minutes)

Phase 1 (3–4 minutes)

Examiner Now, in this part of the test you are going to talk together.
Show Test 2 visuals (page 77) to both candidates.
Here are some pictures that show different sports.
Do you like these different sports? Say why or why not. I'll say that again.
Do you like these different sports? Say why or why not.
All right? Now, talk together.

Candidates ....
Allow a minimum of 1 minute (maximum of 2 minutes) before moving on to the following questions.

Examiner / Do you think …
Candidates … cycling is dangerous?
Use as appropriate. … playing football is fun?
Ask each candidate … playing tennis is exciting?
at least one … running is boring?
question. … playing basketball is interesting?

> **Optional prompts**
> Why?/Why not?
>
> What do **you** think?

Examiner So, Candidate A, which of these sports do you like best?
And you, Candidate B, which of these sports do you like best?
Thank you. (Can I have the visuals, please?)
Retrieve the visuals.

Phase 2 (Up to 2 minutes)

Examiner Now, which sports are most fun to watch on television, Candidate B? (Why?)
And what about you, Candidate A? (Which sports are most fun to watch on television?) (Why?)
How can sports help you make friends, Candidate A?
And you, Candidate B? (How can sports help you make friends?) (Why?)

Thank you. That is the end of the test.

Test 3 Speaking Part 1

(3–4 minutes)

Phase 1

| | | **Back-up prompts** |

Examiner What's your name, please?
To each candidate How old are you?
in turn Where are you from? Are you from (Mexico)?

Phase 2

Back-up prompts

Examiner Now, let's talk about different times of the year.

Candidate A, what seasons are there during the year in your country? Are there four seasons in your country?

Which time of year is special in your country? Is New Year a special time in your country?

Candidate B, when are the school holidays in your country? Do you have school holidays in August?

What is the weather usually like in December in your country? Is it usually cold here in December?

Back-up questions

Extended Response Now, Candidate A, please tell me something about your favourite time of the year.

Do you like the summer?
Do you spend time with family at this time of the year?
Do you go somewhere nice at your favourite time of year?

Back-up prompts

Now, let's talk about food.

Candidate B, who cooks the food in your family? Do you cook for your family?

What kind of food do you eat every week? Do you eat vegetables every week?

Candidate A, what are the cafés like in your town? Are there any good cafés in your town?

Where does your family buy food from? Does your family buy food from a market?

Back-up questions

Extended Response Now, Candidate B, please tell me something about a meal that you enjoy eating.

Do you have this meal with your family?
Who makes it?
Do you often eat this meal?

Speaking Part 2

(5–6 minutes)

Phase 1 (3–4 minutes)

Examiner Now, in this part of the test you are going to talk together.
Show Test 3 visuals (page 154) to both candidates.
Here are some pictures that show different television programmes.
Do you like these different types of television programme? Say why or why not.
I'll say that again.
Do you like these different types of television programme? Say why or why not.
All right? Now, talk together.

Candidates ....
Allow a minimum of 1 minute (maximum of 2 minutes) before moving on to the following questions.

Examiner / Do you think …
Candidates … watching action films on TV is exciting?
Use as appropriate. … watching the news on TV is sad?
Ask each candidate … watching football matches on TV is interesting?
at least one … watching singing on TV is fun?
question. … watching programmes about history on TV is boring?

> **Optional prompts**
> Why?/Why not?
>
> What do **you** think?

Examiner So, Candidate A, which of these television programmes do you like best?
And you, Candidate B, which of these television programmes do you like best?
Thank you. (Can I have the visuals, please?)
Retrieve the visuals.

Phase 2 (Up to 2 minutes)

Examiner Now, do you prefer watching television alone or with other people, Candidate B? (Why?)

And what about you, Candidate A? (Do you prefer watching television alone or with other people?) (Why?)

How much time do you spend watching television on different days of the week, Candidate A? (Why?)

And you, Candidate B? (How much time do you spend watching television on different days of the week?) (Why?)

Thank you. That is the end of the test.

Test 4 Speaking Part 1

(3–4 minutes)

Phase 1

| | | **Back-up prompts** |

Examiner What's your name, please?
To each candidate Where do you live? Do you live in (Guadalajara)?
in turn How many brothers and sister do you have?

Phase 2

Back-up prompts

Examiner Now, let's talk about weekends.

Candidate A, when does the weekend start for you and your family? — Does your weekend start on Friday afternoon?

What do you usually do at the weekend? — Do you play any sports at the weekend?

Candidate B, what will you do next weekend? — Are you going to meet your friends next weekend?

Do all of your family have free time every weekend? — Do your parents have free time every weekend?

Back-up questions

Extended Response Now, Candidate A, please tell me what you did last weekend.
- Did you meet your friends last weekend?
- Did you go anywhere?
- Did you eat anything special last weekend?

Back-up prompts

Now, let's talk about transport.

Candidate B, how do you like to travel if you are going on a long journey? — Do you like long journeys by plane?

How often do you ride a bike in your town? — Do you ride a bike in your town every week?

Candidate A, what do you like about travelling by train? — Do you like reading when you are travelling by train?

How often are there traffic delays in your town? — Are the roads very busy in your town?

Back-up questions

Extended Response Now, Candidate B, please tell me something about how you travelled to school yesterday.
- Did you go to school by car?
- Did you travel to school with your friends?
- Did your journey to school take a long time?

Speaking Part 2

(5–6 minutes)

Phase 1 (3–4 minutes)

Examiner Now, in this part of the test you are going to talk together.
Show Test 4 visuals (page 154) to both candidates.
Here are some pictures that show different places to eat.
Do you like these different places to eat? Say why or why not. I'll say that again.
Do you like these different places to eat? Say why or why not.
All right? Now, talk together.

Candidates ....
Allow a minimum of 1 minute (maximum of 2 minutes) before moving on to the following questions.

Examiner / Do you think …
Candidates … eating at fast food restaurants is healthy?
Use as appropriate. … having a picnic in the park is cheap?
Ask each candidate … eating at school is fun?
at least one … going to a restaurant with your family is fun?
question. … eating at home is boring?

> **Optional prompts**
> Why?/Why not?
>
> What do **you** think?

Examiner So, Candidate A, which of these places to eat do you like best?
And you, Candidate B, which of these places to eat do you like best?
Thank you. (Can I have the visuals, please?)
Retrieve the visuals.

Phase 2 (Up to 2 minutes)

Examiner Now, what's your favourite café or restaurant in this area, Candidate B? (Why?)
And what about you, Candidate A? (What's your favourite café or restaurant in this area?) (Why?)
How often do you and your family go to a café or restaurant, Candidate A?
And you, Candidate B? (How often do you and your family go to a café or restaurant?)

Thank you. That is the end of the test.

Test 5 Speaking Part 1

(3–4 minutes)

Phase 1

| | | **Back-up prompts** |

Examiner What's your name, please?
To each candidate Where are you from?   Are you from (China)?
in turn   Which school do you go to?

Phase 2

Back-up prompts

Examiner Now, let's talk about reading.
Candidate A, how often do you read for fun?   Do you read for fun every day?
What kind of things do your friends like reading?   Do your friends read a lot of books?
Candidate B, what was the last thing that you read online?   Have you read any emails today?
How old were you when you learnt to read?   Could you read when you were six years old?

Back-up questions

Extended Response Now, Candidate A, please tell me about something that you have enjoyed reading.   Have you read a good book this year?
Was it interesting?
Will you read it again in the future?

Back-up prompts

Now, let's talk about the internet.
Candidate B, what can you learn on the internet?   Can you learn English on the internet?
Do you prefer using a phone or a computer to go on the internet?   Do you prefer using your phone to go on the internet?
Candidate A, how often do you chat online with your friends?   Do you use the internet to speak to your friends every week?
What do you like doing most on the internet?   Is watching videos your favourite thing to do on the internet?

Back-up questions

Extended Response Now, Candidate B, please tell me something about what you like doing on the internet.   Is the internet a good way to watch films?
Have you ever bought something on the internet?
Will you use the internet this weekend?

Speaking Part 2

(5–6 minutes)

Phase 1 (3–4 minutes)

Examiner Now, in this part of the test you are going to talk together.
Show Test 5 visuals (page 155) to both candidates.
Here are some pictures that show different holidays.
Do you like these different types of holiday? Say why or why not. I'll say that again.
Do you like these different types of holiday? Say why or why not.
All right? Now, talk together.

Candidates ....
Allow a minimum of 1 minute (maximum of 2 minutes) before moving on to the following questions.

Examiner / Do you think …
Candidates
Use as appropriate. … staying at a campsite is fun?
Ask each candidate … lying on a beach is boring?
at least one … going to stay with family is cheap?
question. … having a holiday in the mountains is difficult?
… going on a school trip is exciting?

> **Optional prompts**
> Why?/Why not?
>
> What do **you** think?

Examiner So, Candidate A, which of these holidays do you like best?
And you, Candidate B, which of these holidays do you like best?
Thank you. (Can I have the visuals, please?)
Retrieve the visuals.

Phase 2 (Up to 2 minutes)

Examiner Now, is it more fun to have holidays with family or with friends, Candidate B? (Why?)

And what about you, Candidate A? (Is it more fun to have holidays with family or with friends?) (Why?)

Do you ever feel tired after a holiday, candidate A? (Why?)

And you, Candidate B? (Do you ever feel tired after a holiday?) (Why?)

Thank you. That is the end of the test.

Test 6 Speaking Part 1

(3–4 minutes)

Phase 1

Examiner
To each candidate in turn

What's your name, please?
Where do you live?
What is your date of birth?

Back-up prompts

Do you live in (Shanghai)?
When is your birthday?

Phase 2

Examiner

Now, let's talk about learning languages.
Candidate A, what other languages can you learn at your school?
When did you start learning English?

Candidate B, how many English teachers have you had at your school?
What do you find difficult about learning English?

Back-up prompts

Can you learn any other languages at your school?
Did you start learning English when you were nine?
Have you had two different English teachers at your school?
Do you find English grammar difficult?

Extended Response

Now, Candidate A, please tell me something about an English lesson which you enjoyed.

Back-up questions

Was this lesson fun?
Did this lesson happen this term?
Did you learn a lot in the lesson?

Back-up prompts

Now, let's talk about watching things on the internet.
Candidate B, how often do you watch things on the internet?
What kinds of things on the internet make you laugh?
Candidate A, what kind of music videos do you like watching on the internet?
How often have you seen your friends in online videos?

Do you watch online videos every day?
Are there a lot of funny things to see on the internet?
Do you watch a lot of pop music videos online?
Have you ever seen your friends in online videos?

Back-up questions

Extended Response

Now, Candidate B, please tell me about something good that you watched on the internet.

Did you watch this on your own or with a friend?
Would you like to watch the thing that you saw again?
Do your friends often send you things to watch online?

Speaking Part 2

(5–6 minutes)

Phase 1 (3–4 minutes)

Examiner Now, in this part of the test you are going to talk together.
Show Test 6 visuals (page 155) to both candidates.
Here are some pictures that show different places to go shopping.
Do you like these different places to go shopping? Say why or why not. I'll say that again.
Do you like these different places to go shopping? Say why or why not.
All right? Now, talk together.

Candidates ....
Allow a minimum of 1 minute (maximum of 2 minutes) before moving on to the following questions.

Examiner / Do you think …
Candidates … department stores are useful?
Use as appropriate. … markets are cheap?
Ask each candidate … clothes shops are interesting?
at least one … shopping centres are exciting?
question. … supermarkets are boring?

Optional prompts
Why?/Why not?

What do **you** think?

Examiner So, Candidate A, which of these places to go shopping do you like best?
And you, Candidate B, which of these places to go shopping do you like best?
Thank you. (Can I have the visuals, please?)
Retrieve the visuals.

Phase 2 (Up to 2 minutes)

Examiner Now, do you prefer to go shopping on your own or with someone else, Candidate B? (Why?)
And what about you, Candidate A? (Do you prefer to go shopping on your own or with someone else?) (Why?)
What's the best way to buy things cheaply, Candidate A? (Why?)
And you, Candidate B? (What's the best way to buy things cheaply?) (Why?)

Thank you. That is the end of the test.

Test 3 | Visuals

Do you like these different types of television programme? Say why or why not.

Test 4 | Visuals

Do you like these different places to eat? Say why or why not.

Test 5 Visuals

Do you like these different types of holiday? Say why or why not.

Test 6 Visuals

Do you like these different places to go shopping? Say why or why not.

Sample Answer Sheet for Reading and Writing

OFFICE USE ONLY - DO NOT WRITE OR MAKE ANY MARK ABOVE THIS LINE

Cambridge Assessment English

- Candidate Name
- Centre Name
- Examination Title
- Candidate Signature
- Candidate Number
- Centre Number
- Examination Details
- Assessment Date

Supervisor: If the candidate is ABSENT or has WITHDRAWN shade here ○

Key for Schools Reading and Writing Candidate Answer Sheet

Instructions
Use a PENCIL (B or HB).
Rub out any answer you want to change with an eraser.

For Parts 1, 2, 3 and 4:
Mark ONE letter for each answer.
For example: If you think A is the right answer to the question, mark your answer sheet like this:

For Part 5:
Write your answers clearly in the spaces next to the numbers (25 to 30) like this:

| 0 | E N G L I S H |

Write your answers in CAPITAL LETTERS.

Part 1	Part 2	Part 3	Part 4
1 A B C	7 A B C	14 A B C	19 A B C
2 A B C	8 A B C	15 A B C	20 A B C
3 A B C	9 A B C	16 A B C	21 A B C
4 A B C	10 A B C	17 A B C	22 A B C
5 A B C	11 A B C	18 A B C	23 A B C
6 A B C	12 A B C		24 A B C
	13 A B C		

Part 5

25 _____ 26 _____ 27 _____
28 _____ 29 _____ 30 _____

Continues over →

OFFICE USE ONLY - DO NOT WRITE OR MAKE ANY MARK BELOW THIS LINE

REPRODUCED WITH THE PERMISSION OF CAMBRIDGE ASSESSMENT ENGLISH
© UCLES 2019

Photocopiable

Sample Answer Sheet for Reading and Writing

OFFICE USE ONLY - DO NOT WRITE OR MAKE ANY MARK ABOVE THIS LINE

Part 6: Write your answer below.

Examiner's use only
0 1 2 3 4 5

Part 7: Write your answer below.

Examiner's use only
0 1 2 3 4 5

OFFICE USE ONLY - DO NOT WRITE OR MAKE ANY MARK BELOW THIS LINE

REPRODUCED WITH THE PERMISSION OF CAMBRIDGE ASSESSMENT ENGLISH
© UCLES 2019

Sample Answer Sheet for Listening

Draft

OFFICE USE ONLY - DO NOT WRITE OR MAKE ANY MARK ABOVE THIS LINE   Page 1 of 1

Cambridge Assessment English

Candidate Name:
Candidate Number:
Centre Name:
Centre Number:
Examination Title:
Examination Details:
Candidate Signature:
Assessment Date:

Supervisor: If the candidate is ABSENT or has WITHDRAWN shade here ○

Key for Schools Listening Candidate Answer Sheet

Instructions
Use a PENCIL (B or HB).
Rub out any answer you want to change with an eraser.

For Parts 1, 3, 4 and 5:
Mark ONE letter for each answer.
For example: If you think A is the right answer to the question, mark your answer sheet like this: 0 [A● B○ C○]

For Part 2:
Write your answers clearly in the spaces next to the numbers (6 to 10) like this:
0 | ENGLISH
Write your answers in CAPITAL LETTERS.

Part 1
1. A B C
2. A B C
3. A B C
4. A B C
5. A B C

Part 2 (Do not write below here)
6. ___ 6 1 0
7. ___ 7 1 0
8. ___ 8 1 0
9. ___ 9 1 0
10. ___ 10 1 0

Part 3
11. A B C
12. A B C
13. A B C
14. A B C
15. A B C

Part 4
16. A B C
17. A B C
18. A B C
19. A B C
20. A B C

Part 5
21. A B C D E F G H
22. A B C D E F G H
23. A B C D E F G H
24. A B C D E F G H
25. A B C D E F G H

OFFICE USE ONLY - DO NOT WRITE OR MAKE ANY MARK BELOW THIS LINE   Page 1 of 1

Draft

REPRODUCED WITH THE PERMISSION OF CAMBRIDGE ASSESSMENT ENGLISH
© UCLES 2019

Photocopiable

Sample Answer Sheets

Acknowledgements

Our highly experienced team of Trainer writers, in collaboration with Cambridge English Language Assessment reviewers, have worked together to bring you *A2 KEY for Schools Trainer 1*.

We would like to thank Annie Broadhead (writer), Anthony Cosgrove (writer), Helen Garside (writer), Claire Wijayatilake (writer), Carole Bartlett (reviewer), Joanna Kosta (reviewer) and Diane Reeve (reviewer) for their work on the material.

Author

The authors and publishers acknowledge the following sources of copyright material and are grateful for the permissions granted. While every effort has been made, it has not always been possible to identify the sources of all the material used, or to trace all copyright holders. If any omissions are brought to our notice, we will be happy to include the appropriate acknowledgements on reprinting and in the next update to the digital edition, as applicable.

Text

T3: Text about Gaurika Singh. Copyright © Gaurika Singh. Reproduced with permission of Garima Rana Singh; **T5**: Text about Mikaila Ulmer. Copyright © Mikaila Ulmer. Reproduced with permission; Text about Noa Mintz. Copyright © Noa Mintz. Reproduced with permission; Text adapted from "Teenage fashion designer Isabella Rose Taylor spills all about her PBteen collection". Copyright © Bauer Publishing. Reproduced with permission.

Photographs

The following images are sourced from Getty Images.

T1: filadendron/E+; Hero Images; Fred Stein Archive/Archive photos; Bob Thomas/Bob Thomas Sports Photography; Youen Grall/EyeEm; jabejon/iStock/Getty Images Plus; Jeff Greenberg/Universal Images Group; **T2**: Yasser Chalid/Moment; KidStock/Blend Images; Inti St Clair/Blend Images; Chris Ryan/OJO Images; Ute Grabowsky/Photothek; Thierry Monasse/Getty Images News; duncan1890/E+; ugurhan/E+; **T3**: Jean-Yves Ruszniewski/Corbis Sport; John G. Zimmerman/Sports Illustrated; Jonathan Leibson/Getty Images Entertainment; **T4**: Colin Anderson/Blend Images; yulkapopkova/E+; Jonny Basker/DigitalVision; Squaredpixels/E+; ac productions/Blend Images; **T5**: J. Kempin/Getty Images Entertainment; PhotoAlto/Brand X Pictures; UpperCut Images; Noam Galai/WireImage; **T6**: Pete Saloutos/Image Source; Alan Bailey; Henn Photography/Cultura; gorodenkoff/iStock/Getty Images Plus.

The following images are sourced from other libraries:

T1: West Yorkshire Images/Alamy Stock Photo; cover image of Diary of a Wimpy Kid by Jeff Kinney. Copyright © Abrams Books; **T3**: © Rajendra Chitrakar; **T5**: © Mikaila Ulmer.

Commissioned photography by Trevor Clifford Photography and QBS Learning.

Illustrations by QBS Learning.

Audio recordings by DN and AE Strauss Ltd. Engineer: Neil Rogers; Editor: James Miller; Producer; Dan Strauss. Recorded at Half Ton Studios, Cambridge.